I don't suppose you have to believe in ghosts to know that we are all haunted, all of us, by things we can see and feel and guess at, and many more things that we can't.
— Beth Gutcheon

1

Also from Robert W. Parker
Louisville Ghost Walks
Haunted Louisville (2007)
Haunted Louisville 2: Beyond Downtown (2010)

Acknowledgements:

I'd like to recognize and thank dear friends, fellow ghost hunter enthusiasts, and authors, Lonnie and Roberta Brown. The Browns have journeyed with me across the countryside and into homes and locations to hear ghost stories and interviews. The Browns have read and re-read each story and offered suggestions to make each story better for the reading audience. I'd like to recognize and thank my photographer friend Justin Coulter, who joined me on my second book as the senior photographer, and who eagerly volunteered to be my photographer for my third book. Thank you Justin for your time and photography abilities. And last, I'd like to say thank you to each person mentioned in this book who graciously welcomed me into their home, business, or property and shared with me their own, personal ghost stories. And as the title suggests, "Haunted Louisville 3…You're Never Alone" may that thought remain with you as you read and journey through life, that you're never really alone.

HAUNTED LOUISVILLE 3
You're Never Alone

BY ROBERT W. PARKER

A Whitechapel Press Book from Apartment #42 Productions

Original Cover Artwork Designed by
© Copyright 2014 by April Slaughter & Troy Taylor

Original Photographs by Justin Coulter
Editing by Lonnie & Roberta Mae Brown

This Book is Published By:
Whitechapel Press & Apartment #42 Productions
Decatur, Illinois | 1-888-GHOSTLY
Visit us on the internet at http://www.whitechapelpress.com

First Edition – July 2014
ISBN: 1-892523-91-4

Printed in the United States of America

Table of Contents

INTRODUCTION

Louisville Ghost Walks is now in its 12th year of the ghost story tour business. Along the years, as well as along the sidewalks and businesses of downtown Louisville's most famous addresses, guests from just about all 50 states and foreign countries have been enthralled with the history and mystery of this city. With each passing year, the stories have grown and developed with additional ghostly activities to be told.

Quite a few of the stories in this book feature two prominent hotels downtown, the Brown Hotel and the Seelbach Hotel. I've been a guest at both hotels and have experienced on more than one occasion, a ghostly activity or two. Since I begin at the Brown and conclude at the Seelbach, I've gotten to know on a more personal level, several of the employees, who usually have something to tell me about a ghostly encounter or two. I will be presenting the evidence for you, the reader, to draw your own conclusion as to the extent of hauntings in those properties.

Several of the stories told in the book are within easy driving distances, so if you decide to visit for yourself and check out paranormal activities, good luck and may you have happy hauntings. Enjoy reading this collection of stories, and maybe you'll have an encounter of your own one day!

A Ghost of a Christmas Past at the Seelbach

On another one of my evenings prior to going on a walk, I had a conversation with Paul Pleasant, one of the maintenance engineers at the Seelbach. Paul has been at the hotel for about three years now. He usually works the late night shift of the hotel.

"It was last Christmas (December 2010) and we were in the process of returning the Christmas decorations to the 10th floor storage room. I'd got an area adjacent to the 10th floor Grand Ballroom," said Paul.

"I was wrestling about with one of the large Christmas trees and I'd just about gotten it into its storage place. I'd stepped out of the room and was in the foyer. The double doors were open that lead into the Grand Ballroom.

"Something got my attention. I heard a tinkling sound, something like prisms rattling. I stepped into the Grand Ballroom, it wasn't like my eyes playing tricks on me or some thing, but the large chandelier was swaying.

"It wasn't swaying like we were having an earthquake, but something supernatural was causing that chandelier to sway.

"But that wasn't the worst part. I had walked into the Grand Ballroom and was standing near the chandelier, but keep in mind, I wasn't standing under it and looking up.

"I heard this wind blowing, like a huge vacuum cleaner sound. The draperies at the windows, all started to just move, as if a large fan was blowing air in the room. Nothing like that was happening at all. There were no large fans or any type of a ventilation system that would have caused the draperies to blow.

"It appeared to be in a circular motion and all the fabric was the draperies was being blown in the same rotation. Within a minute, the whirlpool of wind stopped. The draperies fell back into their regular hanging position and the chandelier had stopped moving.

"I wasted no time in getting out of the Grand Ballroom. I don't know if something stirred up that spirit when I had brought us the Christmas decorations and trees or not. Now when I'm in that area, I make sure someone else is with me."

Advice Giving Ghost at Miss C's Café at the Henry Clay

I've been a part of the Louisville Convention and Visitor's Bureau for several years. The organization supports Louisville Ghost Walks. On occasion, I'm invited to participate in promotional events in the city. I attended one such event in the winter of 2011. It was on that occasion that I met Andrea Van Nuss, who is employed in management at the Henry Clay in downtown Louisville. We struck up a conversation and I told her about Louisville Ghost Walks. I asked her if she knew if the Henry Clay was haunted. Her response was just about what I expected, there were no ghosts and that if it was haunted, she hadn't heard any reports. She did invite me down to tour the building and just get a general feel of the building. I was thrilled with the invitation to see this grand building in all its restored opulence. I showed up for my scheduled appointment. To my surprise, Andrea wasn't available for the personal tour, but as luck would have it, my tour was led by the building owner's son, Lee Weyland. Lee provided me with a wonderful tour of the building, which in our case, consisted of the basement, and continuing up to the fourth floor. Today, the upper floors of the building are used as residential housing and apartments. My tour consisted of the lobby, public areas and history of the building.

The Henry Clay occupies the corner of Third Street and Chestnut. It is a majestic building that over the decades has had several identities. The main entrance is located at 604 South Third Street. The architectural firm of Joseph and Joseph designed the building. The building is an outstanding example of the neo-classical revival.

In 1924, the Elks Athletic Club Lodge opened as a gentleman's fraternity club. What made it so popular was the fact that even though Prohibition was in full swing, the Elks Lodge was immune from the laws of the land concerning alcohol consumption. The members of the Elks Lodge could raise a toast and share a beverage among brothers, all within the safety of the secret lodge. Then, the members could retreat upstairs and take slumber in one of the many dormitory rooms and leave refreshed for the next day. Once Prohibition was repealed, the grand old building didn't hold the luster it once did, since the members of the Elks Lodge, and everyone in society, could drink in public. The Elks Lodge enjoyed its heyday until 1927.

The next shingle to hang on the building was that of the Henry Clay Hotel. The Henry Clay Hotel received guests until it ceased operation in 1963.

During the 1960s and 70s, the building housed the YWCA. It also served many social needs for the community at the time, such as a clinic for teenage parents, a rape relief center and spouse abuse refuge. In 1988, the YWCA closed its doors and relocated elsewhere in the city.

In November of 1989, the Center for Women and Families took possession of the former grand lodge and athletic center. The Center eventually surrendered the property and moved elsewhere, leaving another abandoned building in the downtown Louisville landscape.

Soon, dust and debris accumulated around the doorways and water damaged the once beautiful ballrooms and gymnasium. The building was a heated topic for years within the city government, of what would become of the former Henry Clay Hotel.

Today, Bill Weyland, owner of City Properties, has restored the grand piece of property and it's used as a stunning event venue, and a residential facility for those who enjoy downtown living in luxury.

I thanked Lee Weyland for his time and knowledge of history and the tour. Prior to departing the property, I asked Lee about any stories concerning ghosts, and his answer was "none that he was aware of." I departed the property, grateful for the tour and presentation, nonetheless.

Two or three weeks later, I got an email from Andrea Van Nuss. Her email was just what I wanted to read.

On the Chestnut Street side, is a small restaurant that operates under the name of Miss C's. The two proprietors, Charlotte and Chris, opened the lunchtime eatery in August of 2010. I wasted no time at introducing myself to the two ladies. I explained my purpose for the visit, and that my calling was prompted by receiving the email from Andrea Van Nuss. The ladies had expressed to Andrea, that their restaurant was 'haunted.'

I made an appointment with Charlotte and Chris for an interview with the two ladies who operate Miss C's. On this warm, summer time day, my friends, Lonnie and Roberta Brown, joined me for lunch at the restaurant.

The lunch crowd began to empty out. Charlotte joined us at our table. It wasn't long until we were laughing, sharing stories, and talking ghosts. Charlotte wasn't a stranger to ghosts and she shared with us some of her personal encounters over the course of her life.

"Chris and I were just having a general, business discussion of whether we should keep open our Butchertown location, or should we just concentrate here, should we keep both places, or try to combine everything. Nobody was here, so Chris and I were just cleaning and talking, and kicking ideas back and forth.

"Unknown to me, Chris had gone to the bathroom. I was busy mopping the floor, just right over here. I'm just mopping and moving the chairs around, and I could tell, it was a man's hand, and he put his hands on the back of my neck. I could tell it was a man's hand by the size.

"It was so plain, and I could feel the hand pressure, and it was like he was bending down to me, and he said, 'stay.'

"And then he was just gone. And Chris came around the corner, and she was like, 'What's wrong with you?'

"I know my eyes were as big as saucers, I had goose bumps and tears were running down my check. That's just the way I am, when something paranormal happens around me, sometimes the hair on the back of my neck will go up, my face will get all flushed.

"It wasn't anything weird, creepy or ominous; it was kind of nice, and I thought, *Oh, real big hands* and I thought, *Oh, that's really kind of nice,"* Charlotte laughed.

"We were just trying to concentrate on whether which location to work with and keep open. It was just running us ragged. And just after he said that, 'stay' things just kind of went into play, and that's exactly what we're going to do. Stay. We're going to build a kitchen here, and the city has loosened up some money for us to stay down here at the Henry Clay."

I asked Charlotte, if she had ever felt anything weird, or menacing, with being alone here at any time.

"I've never felt anything bad here, and I don't think I will. And after that day, maybe he feels at home here in the restaurant. Maybe he just did his little job and said his message. It was very clear."

"Can you think of anything else that has happened to make you think this place is haunted?" I asked Charlotte.

"The first thing we do each morning is make our simple syrup in a real, thick glass measuring cup. The water here is really hot, and we always keep this measuring cup on the shelf in the kitchen. I said to Chris, 'Where's the glass-measuring cup?'

"She answered back that she didn't know. It was last seen on the shelf where we always keep it. It wasn't there.

"We looked all over, everywhere, and couldn't find it anywhere. Chris looked, and I looked; it was gone. Then, about one hour later, I looked up, and it was on the shelf, just where it always set.

"Neither of us had moved it to that location.

"Things always do show up just when you need them.

"Now this really did freak me out; it bothered me quite a bit. At first, I thought, it was a burglar, or a prank, not a ghost, but things sure did change.

"About two weeks ago, I came in on Monday morning, I knew the Henry Clay hosted a prom over the weekend for Fern Creek High School. I was here alone that morning, and I needed to use a knife. I went to get one of Chris' Henckel knives, and I couldn't find it. I thought, *Oh, my gosh, her knife is gone.*

"I thought maybe I was in a hurry and knocked something off, moved it, but I just couldn't find the knife that I needed. I decided there was no use in calling her at the commissary and upsetting her. I just thought the professional knife is gone.

"When Chris showed up, I told her the knife was missing; it was gone. We looked some more, and finally gave up and just reached the conclusion, someone swiped that knife.

"Not knowing what else to do, we contacted Ed. He's the guy who handles security. I told him that one of Chris' knives was gone and it had to have been someone from the prom. He said everything was locked and the kids weren't down here. That wasn't what I wanted to hear. Nobody down here, then where is her knife?

"Sarah, another employee here in the building came down, and she just casually said, 'What's that under the shelf?'

"It was the knife! Now, here's the strangest part that is creepy, but on the tip of the knife, it was a piece of dried up chicken skin! We don't prepare or cook chicken here, food is fixed at the commissary and there would be no reason for chicken skin to be used on a knife.

"I'd looked there, and all around the shelving units, cabinets; you name it, I looked. Chris had crawled about the kitchen as well, and that knife was just laying there, in plain view. It's still a mystery to us as to how that knife ended up there.

"As I said earlier, things just disappear, and they eventually show up, just when we need them. It's like when we were trying to make a business decision about whether to stay here or relocate, and that ghost, well, he just showed up when I needed help making a decision. He told us to 'stay' and we've got no plans to go elsewhere."

An Amorous Ghost at the Seelbach

On one occasion that I was staying at the hotel, I needed a ride to another location in the city. I asked if one of the shuttle drivers would be available to provide me with transportation. My driver that night was named Chevy, a young, tall, early twenty- year old man who had been with the hotel for about one year. The two of us were riding in the shuttle van just making casual talk. He knows I own Louisville Ghost Walks and told the stories in the hotel.

As with most people, the topic of ghosts and hauntings come up. "Chevy, have you ever experienced anything paranormal in the hotel? Or, have you talked with any guests who have experienced something that just couldn't be explained?" I asked him.

"No, I've not had anything paranormal," he started. "However, I heard one thing from a female guest a little while back."

"Go on, what have you heard?" I asked.

"One of the ladies who I was driving to the airport, was telling me about a ghost, who seemed to make some sexual passes at her in the bed. Is that possible? I thought, she must have had too much to drink or something, or some wild dream," he chuckled as he shared that with me.

I wanted to help him and give him the best answer possible. "Chevy, a ghost will return with the same personality that it had in life. So, it is possible that the guest you speak of, could have been sexual accosted as she slept if that particular male ghost found the guest to be sexually attractive. It's not that unlikely.

The Seelbach Hotel

"Can you provide me with any details that she shared with you about that encounter?"

"She was a little tense when she got into the shuttle, and I asked her if she enjoyed her stay. She only stayed one night here. She spoke of the normal stuff, the beauty of the hotel, food, but her tone changed suddenly. She said she wouldn't stay the night at the hotel, ever again.

"I glanced up in the rear view mirror, and just asked, 'Did something go wrong?'

"She moved about in her seat, and said, 'Yeah, this hotel is haunted, and the ghost is very aggressive....and she paused...and said, aggressive sexually.'

"She wasn't laughing or smiling. I couldn't believe what she said, but asked her to tell me what happened if she felt comfortable doing so.

"She said that the room just had a feel about it, like she wasn't alone.

"She got ready for bed, and something was in the bed with her. Something kept touching her on the shoulder, much like it was a hand, then it was on her hips, legs, and she'd move, and turn over in the bed. Then, it would go away, and then, it felt like a hand was moving up and down her body.

"I could tell, she didn't like talking about it. I kept looking at her in the rear view mirror, and it was obviously upsetting her. So, once she stopped talking about it, I never brought it up anymore, and by then, we were at the airport.

"I really don't think she was making this up, or had been drinking too much and it was a nightmare. She experienced something that night that really made an impression on her."

An Unwelcomed Seelbach Guest

Before each walk, I always step inside of the Seelbach Hotel just to make sure there is no convention or meeting occupying the area on the mezzanine level where I present. I don't enjoy those kinds of surprises.

On this particular night in October, one of the night desk clerks named Peter Smith motioned for me to come over. As I crossed past the lobby furniture to meet him, he leaned forward, over the desk. He had look on his face as if he had something exciting to tell me. He glanced left and right, just to make sure nobody was within hearing range.

"The other night, I was working the desk, and the lobby was deserted," he said. "It was between 11 PM and midnight. It was so quiet here, nobody was around, and I could hear just about every sound that his old building was making.

"The elevator doors opened up and this couple got off. They were carrying their luggage. I'd recognized them! Earlier this evening, I'd checked them into the hotel and here they came with their luggage.

"I knew something was wrong.

"I tried to greet them, but the gentleman raised up his hand, as if to stop any pleasantries.

"The gentleman began to speak. He held his wife's hand. 'I've been a Baptist preacher for more than twenty years, and my wife and I are not staying the night in a haunted hotel room!'

"I finally got the couple to calm down and tell me what had happened. He said to me that his wife was lying in the bed watching television. One lamp was turned on. He was just moving about the room and the bathroom,

18

The Grand Lobby Staircase in the Seelbach Hotel

getting ready for bed, too. They were just talking about the day's events and plans for tomorrow.

"He said that he looked at his wife, and her eyes were as wide as saucers and her chin had dropped down, opening her mouth. One arm was outstretched and pointing to something at the foot of the bed.

"Then he said, 'I followed my wife's gaze and point, and standing at the foot of our bed, was this ghost!'

"He said she was gray, in a pale color, and was wearing or had this bluish dress or sash tied about her body.

"He and his wife looked at each other, then they turned back and looked at this ghost! Right before their eyes, that ghost just started to fade away until she was gone. She never made a sound or moved in any direction. She just vanished!

"That's when they decided they were going to disappear, too. They packed their bags and wanted to check out.

"I tried everything I could think of to persuade them to stay here. I offered them a new room, a larger suite, and even breakfast coupons, but they wanted none of that. This couple was determined to leave the hotel. They were upset by that ghostly presence.

"Those two left the Seelbach, and went over to the Marriott to stay the night."

*Author's note....I realize that all of the stories found in my book **Haunted Louisville 3...You're Not Alone** features stories from the local area. However, on one of the nights before a ghost walk, one of my guests had a ghost story she wanted to tell me. Even though my guest is a Louisvillian and we were seated at the Brown Hotel, I felt compelled to include the next story she told me. I hope you'll enjoy it and gain a deeper understanding of the 'power of the paranormal.'*

Because She Breathed Me In

"This goes back to the horrific day of September 11, 2001 that rocked our country," said my guest.

"My sister was working at the World Trade Tower that day when the airplanes struck the building. Just as what we saw on the newscasts, debris was flying every where and people were running for their lives.

"Thank God, my sister survived that attack. She had to under go some therapy from the attack, but with a talented and compassionate counselor, she was able to heal from the events of that day, both emotionally and physically.

"It wasn't too long before she began having nightmares and some disturbing thoughts about that day. Something was robbing her of her peace, and restlessness took over. She wasn't able to eat or sleep well, and began suffering from the stress of the event.

"Back into counseling she returned, but this time it wasn't as successful. The more she spoke of it, the more restless she grew and the nightmares returned.

"A friend just happened to mention to her to try a medium, just to see if there was more to this restlessness and nightmares than what was on the surface.

"'My sister responded in surprise, 'Ghosts? A spirit?' and thought no more of it.

"Since she wasn't getting any relief from the counselor, or at her church, as time passed she decided to contact that medium. She had nothing else to lose.

"She made the appointment with the medium and met her. She relayed the entire experience to her, and spoke in details of the restlessness and nightmares.

"The medium was able to identify that spirits had attached themselves to my sister. Most of the spirits that were present, were harmless, benign spirits, with the exception of one.

"The medium began her work, trying to communicate with the spirit, who happened to be a male who perished on September 11.

"During the session, the medium would ask questions, and a male voice responded from my sister's mouth.

"The male voice said, 'I was in the World Trade Tower the day the airplane rammed into the tower. I was killed instantly along with my coworkers that day. I don't remember falling; I don't remember pain; I just remember that I was dead and I didn't know what to do.'

"The medium asked the male, 'Why did you chose this woman to attach yourself to?'

"The male voice replied, 'Because she breathed me in.'

"Apparently, my sister was running for her life and had stopped long enough to catch her breath, and one time she turned around to see the building ablaze, and with a gasp of air, possibly, she breathed him in. His spirit must have been in such a state of transition and confusion, he was breathed into my sister.

"The medium continued and asked the male spirit, 'Why don't you leave?'

"'Because I can't; I don't know where to go, I'm confused.' he said.

"The medium suggested that he walk toward the light, go toward the light that is there.

"'I see the light,' he responded. 'The light is growing brighter and larger.'

"'Keep going,' said the medium.

"He spoke in an excited voice, 'I see my coworkers. I see Buddy, and James....and at that time, there was a long pause as if he was remembering. Tears began to stream down my sister's face from the emotion to the man's names of his coworkers. And then he added the most powerful words, 'and we're all dead.'

"Tears continued down my sister's face, and then she just wept out of control. The medium tried to make contact with the man, or at least to try to find out his name, but it was too late. He had made his way to the light and now found peace.

"According to my sister, she had no more nightmares and her restlessness had turned to peace. Her joy for life was restored and she felt like healing had actually happened....not just for her, but for the both of them."

Dining at the Dish on Market with a Ghost

Most Louisville residents who have had any contact with downtown Louisville, knows this name, The Delta Lounge, which was an institute of restaurants on the Market Street corridor. It occupied that same location for almost 50 years, before the owners decided to close the business. Family members didn't want the Delta Lounge anymore, and one thing led to another and it was sold, including the furnishing and all the contents. And that includes one ghost!

The former Delta Lounge has a new identity and it operates under new ownership. Two brothers, Anderson and Marshall Grissom, stand at the helm now, and have renamed it as Dish on Market. It opened for business in July of 2010. So, they have now experienced their own restaurant ownership.

My buddy Michael Risinger and I stumbled upon the restaurant in the fall of 2011. Upon our first visit, one of the brothers, Marshall Grissom happened to stop by the table to see if we were enjoying our meal and drinks. One thing led to another and the topic of history and ghosts came up. Marshall Grissom had no personal ghost story to share with me about the property, but pulled up a chair and joined us. Marshall told us what other employees had told him.

"Ralph handles the ordering and inventory of all the bar and restaurant supplies. Ralph works here alone, late at night.

"He says it is easier to do his job while nobody else is around.

"Of course, the building is locked tight and he's in here alone, sometimes behind the bar, other times in the dining area, and more times that he'd care to admit, down in the basement.

From the balcony at Dish Market

working in the basement, he'll hear footsteps of someone walking, a female, in heels, walking across the dining room.

"He'd go upstairs and look all around, and nobody would be there. The door would all be locked and nothing disturbed.

"On some occasions, he'd hear the footsteps and go upstairs, and of course, not find anyone, but would smell the fragrance of perfume, just hanging the air.

"One of the dishwashers, has told of seeing dishes just 'fly' off the shelf and hit the floor hard. Nothing would break, but the dishes would just take off in mid air as if something would grab them and give them a toss.

"Now we both know, no air ventilation would cause dishes to come flying off, and it's not like the shelf collapsed.

"Some of my employees find things like that to be pretty disturbing, and do not want to be here alone," Marshall said.

"I can understand that as well; the power of the paranormal can be very unnerving," I added.

Marshall told me of one of his long-term employees, Misty Streeter, who said she'd be a good employee to interview. She has had her own, personal encounter with not just any ghost, but the ghost of a family member inside the restaurant.

The Haunted Booth?

I returned one afternoon later in the winter season. Misty said she'd worked at the Delta for a number of years, and she came with the deal for the new owners of Marshall and Anderson Grissom for continued employment.

She had a few minutes and joined me in a booth. I told her that I understood she had a ghost story to share with me. She agreed.

"I've worked here for several years," she began. "My dad was a regular who stopped in here often when he got off from work.

"My dad was a construction worker on several of the buildings downtown. His look never changed. He always wore jeans and flannel shirts.

"He came in here so often, that he had his own booth. It's the fourth one back, along the wall."

I turned and looked over my shoulder, and counted back four booths.

"My dad died suddenly, completely unexpected. It was a shock to my family and me. During the stress, I had taken a couple weeks off to deal with the funeral, paper work that follows, and everything else that comes with a deceased relative.

"I had just returned back to work, thinking he always would drop by in here in the afternoon, usually about 3 PM.

"The bar area was quiet and I had my back to the dining room. I turned and started walking toward the kitchen to get something. Out of the blue, I said, 'I'll be right back, Dad, to get your drink.'

"No sooner than I had said that, I stopped, turned and looked back at the booth. I saw my dad sitting there, well, I saw his back side, his head, back, and shoulders. But I knew in my heart, it was my dad!

"I ran into the kitchen and just started crying. Cindy, the cook came up to me and asked me what was wrong. I said to her, 'I just saw the ghost of my dad sitting in his booth!'

"Cindy went into the bar area, and came back and said, 'Nobody is sitting out there; his booth is empty.'

"I wiped the tears from my eyes and went back into the bar side. Cindy was right; nobody was in the bar. I guess my first reaction was that I saw a man who favored my dad, wearing a flannel shirt. I guess my mind was playing tricks on me, but as I slowly walked to the booth where my dad always sat, nobody was there at all. The booth was empty.

"I know what I saw, and it was the ghost of my dad."

Frazier History Museum's Spirited Ghost

In the 1900s, on the blocks of Main Street between 8th and 12th Streets in downtown were known at Tobacco District when Louisville was enjoying the height of the cash tobacco crop. The building that houses Frazier History Museum has a corner stone marker out front that reads, *Meguiar, Harris and Company*, with two fancy pipes sketched into the stone. This section of the historic Tobacco District is an up and coming area of buildings that have been re-purposed into new and creative uses. Even with new and creative uses, that could make a ghost or two, a little more active as well with all the excitement.

I sing with the Thoroughbred Chorus and on one of the Christmas season nights of 2013, the Thoroughbred Chorus performed at the Frazier History Museum. The Thoroughbred Chorus had finished performing and we had access to tour the museum. I really enjoyed that opportunity to tour the museum, and view the Napoleon Exhibit that was on loan.

The first and second floors were closed off due to the company Christmas party that was in progress. We had access to the upper floors. As I was strolling about the third floor, I was able to have a conversation with one of the security guards that was on duty. Our conversation was centered on the usual attractions and exhibits, but soon it turned to the paranormal that she brought up to me.

"I've lived in haunted houses all my life," the young female security guard began. "So, I'm used to the typical hauntings that happen."

"What do you think of this museum?" I asked her.

The Frazier History Museum

"The entire place is haunted. Especially after dark, with the mannequins and weaponry on display, it's easy to sense the eerie and sinister feeling," she said.

"Yes," I said. "I can feel an uneasy atmosphere."

"You're right, just by looking at the swords and some of the mannequins, and how they are displayed in battle scenes, could make anyone uncomfortable. But, I've gotten used to the displays and I know what's behind each corner, but on occasion, I do get a little *creeped out,* "she said.

"What do you mean by, *creeped out* that you mentioned? What has happened here?" I asked her, as we were strolling about the displays.

"I work the second shift hours, and security is in the building 24/7, and the third shift guys have to do hourly walk-through of the building. They usually walk through the building in the dark, with only the light of flashlights and the security lights overhead. Everything does seem to become just a little more life-like in the dark, and the stillness of the museum creates a new atmosphere.

"I've witnessed this and heard from the other security guards on the third shift, that when we're down in the control room, and the museum is locked, something will trigger the motion detectors. The lights in the control room monitor blink and that indicates something is moving about. But, whatever is moving about, doesn't turn out to be human, ghostly, but not human.

"But, nothing is seen on the video monitors, but something unknown, is causing the motion detectors to blink. We have no choice but to respond to where the lights are blinking, and it's always the third floor, that's the only floor when the monitors seem to act up.

"Of course, nothing is ever found."

"So, you've walked the third floor yourself, responding to the motion detectors?" I asked her.

"Yes, even if the museum closes at the normal time, the motion detectors can go off anytime as if someone is stirring about. But, nobody is ever seen or found.

"A couple years ago, a paranormal research team of investigators came into the building. Their research and investigation showed that the ghost of a little girl was haunting the third floor. The little girl travels all over the third floor and some of their photographs and videos did pick up the shape of a little girl."

"Do you know if the paranormal investigators could determine a time period, or how she was dressed? Or why she could be haunted this building?" I asked my guide.

"They didn't give that much detail, other than it was a female spirit of that a child, and for the most part, she's harmless. I don't think she has anything to do with the museum as an attraction, but she's here because of the building.

"My take of the female ghost of the child is that she is connected to the time period of the tobacco business. You know, all of Jefferson County is smoke free, but on occasion when the monitors go off, there is a faint aroma of cigar or tobacco smell when we come up here to investigate. That's why I feel that she goes back to the era of the tobacco district with this building.

"Now, here's the strangest of all things.

"Be sure to go inside the Napoleon Exhibit. This is the first time that I can recall that a piece of furniture that we have on display has something attached to it."

"What do you mean, something attached to it? Are you saying a ghost has attached itself to a piece of furniture?" I responded to her.

"We have a large dressing table that has a mirror. The dressing table belongs to the Napoleon Exhibit, and in that particular room, the motion detector goes off at all hours of the day and night. The motion detector goes off during the day when we have guests in the museum, but keep in mind no guests would be in or near the dressing table. The exhibits in that area are roped off. Guests can only get so close.

"At night, when we're closed, the motion detector goes off as if something has crossed over the boundary sensor, and, of course, there is nobody there at all."

"People have told me that mirrors are like portals to the other side," I mentioned to her. "Do you know if anyone has seen a reflection in the mirror or not? That might hold some clues!"

"No images that I'm aware of have been seen in the mirror, but it does give me the creeps when I'm back there alone in that display area. There's something attached to the dressing table, but when you think of the age and history of that, it would be hard to believe that nothing was attached to it. Something paranormal possibly, but I like to think that maybe a piece of Napoleon himself, could be following that dressing table around."

Friends Forever with a Ghost From
Southern Middle School

Not many people, who are life-long residents of the south Louisville area, aren't familiar with some of the usual locations of that part of the city. There's the famed Iroquois Park, and tree lined Southern Parkway. If you're tracing history, one can't forget about Churchill Downs, going back to 1875. But beyond the hills of the park and the large homes, and the twin spires, stands a school at the corner of Bellevue and Ashland Avenue, Southern Junior High School. Over the years, it has undergone some name changes, to Southern Middle, to Southern Leadership, and now, Frederick Law Olmsted Academy North.

The school was built in 1922 to serve the students of the south Louisville neighborhood. During the 1937 flood, the school was used as a shelter and Red Cross Hospital. The school saw the student population swell to record numbers, forcing the Louisville City School System to build the addition on the backside. But, none of those accolades compare to the ghost that haunts the building.

Now, not every ghost has to be old or creepy or menacing to the people to whom they make their presence known. Ghosts need to have a connection, or a reason to haunt a building. Southern Middle School, as it was during this time for this story, is no exception for the paranormal.

Pat Driskell, the school's retired secretary, and whose name graces the auditorium, has much to share about the school. Pat would be considered to be the historian for the building. Not only was she an employee, she was also a student.

Southern Middle School

"Now, some people would claim that this is just a pure coincidence, but there have been two deaths associated with room 201. Years ago, teacher Mary Anne Gravis became ill while teaching in that room, and she passed suddenly," stated Pat.

"Then, it was Kim Phelps who started her teaching career at Southern, and she was assigned room 201. Does history actually repeat itself?" Pat mused.

Language Arts teacher, Roberta Brown, served as a member of the Southern Middle faculty for years. She joined the Southern faculty in 1973 and occupied several classrooms during her career there. Roberta retired in 1999.

Roberta shared her experience with me, and it was a great reunion for the two of us, because I taught at Southern Middle. I was acquainted with Kim Phelps.

"If another ghost were to haunt the old Southern Middle School, it should be the ghost of math teacher Charlie Saylor," I added to the conversation I had with Roberta. "He served on the interview committee for the hiring of Kim Phelps, and he had reservations about her, because of her youth."

No matter Charlie's first impression of Kim, she was hired and joined the faculty as a 6th grade teacher on the Southern Stars team.

"Charlie later changed his opinion of Kim in just a matter of weeks. She was respected by the students in no time at all, and embraced by her coworkers. Kim had one of those personalities that just lit up the room, and made people feel welcomed and good," I said.

Roberta told me how she learned that Kim was ill.

"Kim came into my room in February, of 1996, and said, 'I don't want to worry you, but I have to be out for a couple of days. I've been really tired and I have something sticking in my throat. The doctor wants me to go into the hospital to run some tests.

"For Kim, the two days turned into weeks. Once all the tests were completed and the results were studied, it was confirmed that a huge, malignant tumor had wrapped itself around her heart and was growing into her throat, causing the sticking. Everyone was concerned. Teachers would gather to remember Kim in prayer before the start of the school day. Kim returned later in the spring and taught regularly during and after the chemo treatments. When school ended for the school year, everyone wondered what would happen to Kim. Would she be able to return in August?

"Kim faithfully worked at Southern that August. She returned and was prepared for the start of the new year as it was unfolding, 1996-97. The students even in the face of this illness admired her. Kim was a fighter, and she had every intention of winning the battle against cancer. The cancer, even for the strong willed patient, raged in full force against Kim. She never let it slow her down or make her feel discouraged. She had a job to do, and that was to teach, and she planned to carry out her duties till the end.

"Unfortunately, the end came sooner than what Kim or anyone expected. Kim pursued various treatments and explored medical routes, all promising something better. As time would have it, her hair fell out from the medication and chemotherapy. But Kim handled it well, by purchasing wigs and turbans. Even though she grew weaker, in some ways she grew stronger for the people that she was close to. We knew it was a struggle for Kim to remain at school all day. In some cases, she had to call her husband Bob to come and pick up her from school. She tried so hard to be strong, dedicated, for the students and her coworkers.

"I remember once, she left my room one morning and went to the restroom. She didn't return, so I went to check on her. I found her curled up in a fetal position on the floor of the restroom! I sometimes asked her, 'Kim, why don't you just stay home and rest?' She would always say, 'Roberta, I just want my life to be normal again.'

"During the painful ordeal of the cancer treatments, Kim wanted to be told the truth about her condition. Her radiation ended in November, 1996, and they ran tests to see if the cancer was in remission. She made her husband Bob promise to come to school to tell her the results in person regardless of whether they were good or bad.

"At lunch time, we were taking our students to the cafeteria. I was at the head of the line and Kim was at the end. I saw Bob first, standing by the window in the hall at the bottom of the stairs. I could tell by his face that the news was bad. I hurried the students onto the cafeteria. I looked back, and I saw Kim rush into Bob's arms. They started walking toward the office. As soon as the last student was inside the cafeteria, I ran to the office. Kim and Bob were leaving. She was crying and she told me that the radiation hadn't helped. The cancer was still there. She hugged me and they left. That was my last time seeing Kim alive.

"The few remaining weeks of November passed. Kim never returned to school. She had requested no visitors and we honored that request. Cards and notes were mailed to her. Anything that would lift her spirits, we as a faculty and friends tried to do. We just felt like Kim wanted to save her strength to do things with her young daughter and to try to keep things as 'normal' as Kim could. Amazingly enough, sometime during her treatments and time to recoup at home, Kim had managed to select a few Christmas gifts to give. She was always thinking of others.

"I received a phone call from Kim in late November. She told me that the doctors had given her two weeks to get her affairs together before returning to the hospital for massive treatments.

"The call was one thing on her list that she wanted to do. She wanted me to know that she loved me and that my writing to her every day had meant the world to her.

"I told her that I loved her, too, and I think, we spoke of death and what we thought it would be like. Somehow, we managed to get through that conversation without breaking down.

"Soon after she entered the hospital and she never came out. She was in and out of consciousness.

"Her mother told me that on the night of her death, Kim called my name. I don't know what she wanted to say to me. She died in the early hours before daylight.

"It was the final day before Christmas vacation. The date was December 12, 1996. I remember it clearly, and that was the day I saw Kim's ghost.

"The students were walking to their homeroom classes that morning. I was in the hallway monitoring the students. Kim's classroom was directly across the hall from my room. I looked up, and suddenly, Kim was standing there by her door. She was healthy and absolutely radiant. She was so happy to be watching the students go by. That shiny dark hair of hers was flipping around as she turned her head to watch. I moved to Mrs. Klawier's door, which was a neighboring teacher, and said, 'Kim's here.'".

Mrs. Klawier said, "What?"

I replied, "Oh, I know she's not really here. In fact, I'm sure that Kim died last night, but she has come to say good-bye, to have one last day at school with the students."

"Mrs. Klawier turned, looked, but she didn't see the ghost of Kim. Her ghost vanished. Only students traveling in the hallway were present, and we're sure, they didn't see the ghost of Kim either.

"The first hour bell had sounded, and all the students had gathered into their homeroom and first period classes. An announcement came from the office, requesting that one of the Southern Star teachers come to the office for a phone call.

"Our team leader, Mrs. Willinger, went to the office to take the call. I had a feeling that I knew what the phone call was all about.

"When Mrs. Willinger returned, she was crying. I asked her to compose herself first, for I'd already absorbed the shock and knew that Kim had already died by seeing her ghost. The students had seen Mrs. Willinger in tears.

"A student raised his hand and asked, 'Did Mrs. Phelps die?'

"I wasn't going to lie to the students, and told the students that, 'Yes, Mrs. Phelps died last night.'

"At that point, I asked the students to take out their writing journals and to just write about their thoughts, their feelings, anything that came to mind concerning Mrs. Phelps' death.

"The room was quiet, when we heard a knock on the door. It was an office aide, delivering a Christmas present to me.

"The aide said it was a gift to me from Mrs. Phelps.

"We all just gasped and the students stared in disbelief as I held the wrapped package. Someone spoke up and said, 'But she's dead! How could she send you a present?'

"I said, 'Isn't that just like her? Still thinking of us!'

"The students wanted me to open the gift, so I did. It was a little wooden, hand painted Christmas tree. There were red metal candleholders on the tree. There were white candles in a personal tin box of hers that I'd always admired. It had chipmunks and other little animals on it and on the lid, it said, *Friends Forever.* The tree and the little tin box are still in my office. I still think of her every day."

The spirit of Kim Phelps remained at Southern for the remainder of the school year. As with any education program, students come and go, and the calendar pages are removed each month. But, concerning Kim Phelps, I think she left a lasting part of her spirit at Southern Middle School and in the hearts of all who knew her.

Ghost of the Crescent Hill Neighborhood at DiFabio's

One of the great privileges of researching and interviewing property owners and businesses about ghosts is the opportunity to meet all the people that make it possible. Each person seems to have some information, a new twist to share about his neighborhood, or he knows the history which makes the reading more interesting when it comes to connecting with ghosts.

The Crescent Hill neighborhood lies just to the east of the city of Louisville. One source reports that the Crescent Hill neighborhood was named after the city of New Orleans, known as the Crescent City. Another report documents that it was named after resident Catherine Anderson Kennedy, who noted the crescent shape reservoir at Reservoir Park, as she ascended its hill one-day. The third, and most likely the most accurate, referred to the uphill curve of Frankfort Avenue as it rose from Clifton Avenue to the site of the old fairgrounds. No matter its origin, Crescent Hill is primarily a residential area of the city of Louisville.

The main thoroughfare is Frankfort Avenue and still remains the major corridor for transportation of the area. Businesses and homes line Frankfort Avenue and just by mentioning its name, residents in the greater Louisville area know it's still a prestigious address to have.

It wasn't always called Frankfort Avenue. In the early 1800s, Frankfort Avenue was once called Shelbyville Pike. It was a well-used stagecoach road that Native Americans had pretty well established as a route.

In 1817, the main road was upgraded to eliminate the deep wagon ruts and it was renamed the Shelbyville and Louisville Turnpike. Along the route, tollhouses were established.

Note the toll-booth window on the front side

The plan was for tollhouses to be placed about every three to five miles apart. The purpose of the tollhouses was simple. Someone was needed to be responsible for maintaining a specific stretch of road, to keep it free from debris and in a passable condition; otherwise, the road would lose its charter. Operating a tollhouse provided stable employment and housing. One of the benefits was being one of the first to hear all the news and happenings in other towns. Tolls were charged according to the number of passengers and animals using the road. Livestock was to be charged a higher rate than a single horse rider, and wagons were more expensive too, since their wheels could damage the road. Residents of the immediate area used the road for free, as well as soldiers, preachers, and funeral attendees, but travelers were required to pay a small amount for passage, usually about a nickel. Some travelers saved money by traveling at night, in the dark along the deserted roadway. This was acceptable because even the toll housekeeper needed to sleep.

The year was 1830, and the first of such buildings was erected three miles from the Jefferson County Courthouse. It was appropriately named the

DiFabio's Casapela Restaurant

Three-Mile House. Today, its actual address is 2311 Frankfort Avenue, near the intersection of Frankfort and Keats Avenue. The house wasn't known to be architecturally pleasing in design or layout. The red brick structure was built in the shape of an upper case "T" with a long porch on the front to protect the keeper from inclement weather as he collected his tolls.

Families soon began to settle the area. Saloons, livery, and shops soon clustered around the tollhouse. During the late 1840s, the Louisville and Frankfort Railroad Co laid tracks through the community, which changed the area forever. Crescent Hill and Clifton were now linked to the city of Louisville via the railroad.

In January of 2011, my buddy Michael Risinger and I happened to drop by a new Italian restaurant in the Crescent Hill neighborhood by the name of DiFabio's Casapela Italian Restaurant. Expecting to enjoy some wonderful, homemade Italian food served in a great environment, we were not disappointed, yet, little did we know we'd discover another ghost story.

We parked next to the building and passed the glow of the lights from the exterior windows. As we neared the entrance, the sounds of a busy chef in the kitchen echoed. The air was filled with the wonderful aroma of garlic. Stepping inside the front door, we felt like we were inside someone's home. The restaurant has a small entrance foyer, just like one would find in a home. Black and white tile lines the floor and a large, Italian painting is displayed on the wall. On he left side is the dining room. About ten to twelve tables were in this room. The fireplace is the centerpiece with the DiFabio name in mosaic tiles. Ryan served as our host and seated Michael and me at the table. Our waiter arrived at our table and he welcomed us for dinner. He made a recommendation for wine and a chef's appetizer, which we ordered.

"I believe this place is haunted," I commented to Michael. "Just look how old it is, and what is was used for when it was built," I commented as we glanced at our menus.

He placed his wineglass on the table and looked about the dining room, too. We both wondered what this particular room would have been used for, and if this was at one time, a single-family residence. As he and I discussed my feelings on the place being haunted, the waiter overheard our conversation and decided to clear up any confusion or wonderment.

"I've not had any paranormal experiences here, but one of the owners, Caitlind, now she has. She's spoken about a ghost out in the foyer. I'll send her over to speak with you," he said.

Caitlind, her sister Sarah, and Sarah's fiancé Ryan are joint owners in the restaurant. The young, dark haired Italian girl with the pleasant smile sat down at the table. She made us feel very relaxed and we discussed the possibility of the building being haunted.

"Do know think this place is haunted?" I asked her.

"I've had one experience in the building, prior to our opening date," she said.

I interrupted her with a question. "What is the history of this property, because that might be a clue as to who is haunting the building. How long have you been here?"

"We opened in February of 2010. The building, which has a resemblance to a house, had previously been Ray Parella's and before that, a restaurant called Sweet Surrender. We fell in love with the building, and thought it would be a great location and it's already been known in the community as an Italian restaurant.

"I agree with you, it does look like a house, with large windows, a fire place, hallway and all. I could just see a family living here," I told her.

"But from what I understand, it wasn't just a residence," she began.

"How so?" I asked.

"This was the toll house, and not only that, but it was a jail cell, for people who couldn't pay the toll! We use the cell as our beverage and dessert service room. It's located here in the front of the dining room."

The three of us all stood up and walked to a smaller service room in the front. She explained that at one time, this room was the jail cell. We made the assumption that it was probably just a temporary holding cell, and if need be, the police from Louisville could come here and transport any serious criminals into Louisville for booking.

We returned back into the dining room and took our seats again.

Michael refilled our wineglasses and asked Caitlind, "Okay, so how or why do you think the building is haunted?"

"I saw a ghost!" she exclaimed.

"We rented the property in February and had started moving in right away. It was March and I was doing some painting. We'd been moving into the property and doing as much of the labor ourselves.

"I was in the hallway painting around the kitchen doorway. I was facing the front door with my back to the bathrooms and hallway. Nobody else was here at all and I had all the exterior doors locked.

"I kept seeing out of the corner of my eye, a little girl. I'd turn around and look, and nobody was there. The hair on my neck was starting to stand up. I'd look, turn around again, and look for the child, and nobody was there.

"I'd definitely got the feeling that I was being watched and that I wasn't alone.

"I must have stopped and turned around about a dozen times, looking for the little girl that I kept seeing from the corner of my eye. I'd turn around and she'd be gone."

"What did you do, or say, or think? Can you describe her? Did she look pale?" I asked her.

"She appeared to be about five years old, and I could see her in color. Her dress was purple, and her skin color was normal, just like our coloring.

"This is what freaked me out so much, is that she looked so normal."

I asked Caitlind, "Did she appear to be from our time period? Maybe the 1940s or 1950s? Or even earlier in time?"

"Oh, from a long time ago. Definitely, not anytime recently. I'd say the early 1900s. The clothing she was wearing was from a different time period, nothing current for our manner of dress at all. Everything about her made her look old. And as quickly as she came, she just faded away from sight when I'd look for her."

"If you were painting in the foyer, where was she appearing?" I asked.

"She was almost, just right behind me in the area. I'd see her and turn, as if someone had entered the room."

"Did the feel a sudden change in temperature? Did you sense anything?" Michael asked her.

Michael's questions raised some interesting points to consider.

Caitlind addressed us both. "The temperature didn't change, and I didn't feel fearful. At one time, I stopped and put down the brush and I walked about the restaurant, looking for the child. It was so real to me, I just thought someone was here, it was very realistic.

"I checked all the doors and everything was locked, so it wasn't like anyone popped in and ran out. I heard no footsteps, nothing at all.

"It was definitely an odd thing to have experienced."

"Now, this is speculation, but what do you think is the connection of the little girl that you saw as a ghost in the foyer?" I asked her.

"The way I think is she grew up here, and lived here with her family. In a worse case, maybe she died young. Maybe had an early death.

"Now, this is just a side note. I want you to know that I'm familiar with ghosts and paranormal stuff. When I was growing up, my family lived in Ohio, and our house had a ghost. We had a ghost that lived in the attic. We'd hear things moving around up there, and we'd know that nobody was up in the attic. So, here, there was no talking or footsteps heard at all.

"Up in the house in Ohio, we gave the ghost a name, and I believe we named her Anne or Helen. Things would be moved about and we'd ask who moved this or how did this get here. It never bothered me. I thought it was a novelty.

"We stayed in the house for years and eventually we moved away."

"I was curious to see if you'd had any other experiences, or if this was the first time ever," I said to Caitlind.

"With this little girl, I feel like it is more of a curiosity type. She's not here to be vicious or mean. It is almost like a 'who are you and what's going on?'

"This is how I think about it. I've not seen her anymore, so I think she just wanted to check things out and she's gone on her way, back to wherever she came from. I've never felt threatened more curious about the people."

"With your background that you've shared, do you think you'd be scared of the ghosts?" I asked.

"I think it would depend on the ghost, maybe one that is angry with unfinished business. I think that would be it, but just the thought or an idea of a ghost scaring me, no not really.

"The way I look at it, is that some people get caught between the two time periods, or stuck, and sometimes that just leads over into our world."

"And I believe, all we can do is make those ghosts feel welcome, and being in a restaurant, they'll be surrounded by people enjoying good food," I added.

Ghost of Macy's Oxmoor Mall

It's not often that I, as the writer can say that I knew the deceased, before he returned as a ghost. Unfortunately, I never saw the ghostly spirit return, but a colleague sure did see the ghost. And my colleague didn't realize that she was seeing a ghost; she thought it was the real person, in real life.

The location of this story happens to be in an unlikely place, Macy's Department Store in the Oxmoor Mall. I was a Macy's employee on part time status for many years. As I mentioned in the opening paragraph, I knew the deceased who decided to return to work to finish up a few tasks that he wasn't able to complete while he was still 'living.' Here is his story.

Mr. William Wright was one of the full time employees at Macy's Department Store. He'd been hired in shortly after he retired from driving a truck and spent several more years working at the store. William was one of those employees that you could set your watch by, being punctual, faithful, and conscientious to his tasks. His specialty was men's clothing, shirts, ties, and putting the entire outfit together, as well as waiting on customers and providing quality service.

If you've ever worked retail, you would know there are many behind the scene tasks that just seem to never go away. One is refolding dress shirts so they can be returned to the selling floor and be in a presentable way for the next customer. William was a meticulous folder, and when he was finished folding a shirt, you couldn't tell that it had been tried on at all. No detail was left undone.

Another characteristic of William is that he often wore a tape measure about his neck, draped over the shoulders of one of his many cardigan sweaters he would wear.

Macy's Department Store at Oxmoor Mall

If there was a question about something, William would know the answer, or he would find out the answer. William was a dedicated Macy's employee, a no-nonsense kind of guy.

On this particular August morning, William was assigned to open the department and get the cash registers all ready for the morning customers. One of his morning tasks was to go into the back alteration room and begin sorting out and folding dress shirts from the night before. Prior to the store's opening, most of the overhead lights are turned off, and the sales floor is dimly lit. Sometimes, the mannequins even look like real people as you move about in a near dark environment. Day in and day; out William would complete his tasks in a timely manner as he was assigned to do.

This morning became the exception. The store was open for business and William was at the cash register with another sales associate. From what I was told, by the other associate is that William became ill, lost his color, and fell over, collapsing on the floor by the cash register. Even though EMS was called and they hurried to the store, it was just too late. William was pronounced dead.

When I reported to work that evening, of course, I was told the tragic news of William's untimely death. Since I was well acquainted with William,

I spearheaded a collection of money for flowers among other employees. I also visited the funeral home and offered my sympathy to the surviving family members. William would be greatly missed.

Anna Pinkus is another colleague of mine from Macy's. Anna, at that time, was the lead employee in the visual department and merchandising. Anna's work schedule was usually 6:00 AM to 2:00 PM. Anna was one of the few employees who could be found at the store in the wee hours of the morning, and on some occasions, working the late night hours well after the doors were locked.

When Anna shared this with me, it was just a couple of days after William's death and even the burial. I ran into Anna elsewhere in the city and she knew I was into ghost stories and paranormal encounters. Anna was relieved to see me, for she had something that had to be told.

"I heard about William's death after the fact. I couldn't believe he had died so suddenly, and I couldn't believe he'd return, for any reason," Anna began.

"What happened?" I asked Anna.

"I had been off from work for a few days and didn't have any idea about William's death. I go into the store just before 6:00 AM, and only security is there; and maybe some of the custodian workers. Otherwise, I'm alone.

"I was on the second floor dressing some mannequins, and I had a large cart with me that had boxes of new shirts for display. Only a few lights were on in the department, but I'm so used to working in the dark, I never thought anything about it.

"I saw William! I spoke to him, I said something like, 'Good morning, you're here awfully early this morning, aren't you?'

"He was just walking among the rows of dress shirts, just as normal as could be, and he had the tape measure around his neck. He mumbled something back to me as a greeting, and in an audible voice, almost like 'I've got some shirts to fold in the back room' or something like that.

"I didn't really think much more about it, other than it was early and unlikely for a sales associate to be here.

"I had some shirts to display and had moved about in the department with my cart. I could see the light from the alteration room lighting up the hallway. The door was open. I'd glance up and on occasion, see William moving about with shirts in the alteration room.

"A few minutes had passed and I walked past the alteration room to return some neckties to where they belong. I could see William in the alteration room folding shirts. I didn't go inside, I just returned to my cart and continued with my shirts that I was going to display on some front tables.

"Time must have slipped away from me. I'd say it was getting close to 7:30 AM and one of the security guards happened to pass by me like he normal does. He was headed toward the alteration room with keys in his hand. After we spoke, I told him that William was already in the alteration room and was folding shirts. The security guard just stood there and looked at me; then he turned and looked toward the alteration room's door.

"William?" he said, almost surprised. "William who?"

"William, he's back there, our William is folding shirts. I've seen him, and spoke to him. Yeah, he's here early folding shirts."

"William's not here, Anna; William's dead," the guard said to me in a serious tone.

"What? What are you talking about?" I said to him.

"William's in that room folding shirts." By then, I had walked over to where the security guard was standing, which was in close proximity to the hallway that led to the alteration room.

The hallway was dark and no light was shining on tiled floor, nor was the alteration room door opened.

"William was in that room," I said to him, in just about an almost, uneasy sounding voice. I was beginning to doubt myself.

"William died last week here at the store, and he's already been buried. Anna, it couldn't have been William," he said to me.

Then he reached out and put his arm around my shoulder and pulled me in against him. We both just stood there at the hallway.

"Since he had the keys, we walked down the hallway and he unlocked the door. I was just a tad bit apprehensive at opening the door. My mind was still processing the news that William was dead, yet, I'd seen him that morning. How could that be?

"The security guard unlocked and opened the door. He reached inside and turned on the light. The dark room was now flooded in light. A couple silent sewing machines were there, two ironing boards, lots of clothes hanging waiting to be altered, and a few old style dress forms, but no William. Nobody was inside the room, and it looked like nobody had been inside of the room, since yesterday.

"On that table, that's not too far from the doorway, were placed several folded shirts, all neatly stacked in their plastic bags, all ready to be returned to the sales floor."

Halloween Happenings at the Seelbach Hotel

One of my favorite Halloween activities is to gather up some friends, select a costume for myself and attend the 4th Street Live adult Halloween party that is held every year. The year of 2012 was no exception. I had also reserved two rooms at the Seelbach. One that I consider 'my room' which is room 1001, and I reserved the one across the hall for two of my friends, Danny and Julie. I was going to share my room with my buddy Kenny.

As the night passed on, we had gotten separated with the different bars and venues for the party. Shortly after midnight, I had decided to call it a night. I made my way back to the Seelbach Hotel and was ready to relax in my room. I knew Kenny would return at some time, as well as Danny and Julie for the other room.

My plan for the night was based on what had happened the previous year. I wanted to re-enact with the reserving the same room, prepare for bed at about the same time as last year, and sleep in the same bed. I wanted to encourage or invite the ghost who came last year and knocked on the door in the wee hours of the morning.

Keeping with my plan, I prepared for bed, turned out all the lights and settled down for sleep.

Kenny came into the room around 2 AM. That woke me up and I sat up in the bed and asked Kenny about the events of his night. Kenny told me about the strange knocks that were sounded on Danny and Julie's door from earlier in the afternoon.

At Danny and Julie's door, there were knocks. Julie opened the door and nobody was there. Just that little episode put Julie on 'high alert' for any ghostly activity and left her feeling a little uneasy.

The author at the door to the haunted room!

Kenny continued telling me about the costume parties and such as he prepared for bed. In my mind, I was secretly wishing that Kenny would hurry up and turn out the lights, for I was waiting for my 'ghostly visitor' to come knocking on my door. I didn't think the ghost would knock if she heard human voices and saw the lights on.

Kenny finished up in the bathroom and got settled into his bed. All the lights were now off. I must have been weary for I fell right to sleep and remembered nothing else of the night until I heard Kenny call my name around 8 AM that next morning.

"Robert, you awake?" he began.

"Yes," I mumbled.

"Did you hear those voices in the room last night?" he asked.

By then, I was sitting up in my bed and looking his way. Kenny had propped himself up in his bed as placed his pillow in front of him.

"What voices are you talking about?" I asked him.

"Well, it started about 4 AM, at least that was what I thought I could read on the clock. At first, I thought you were talking in your sleep, and that's what woke me up. I said 'what' and you never answered.

"I just laid in the bed and thought, you're really having some conversation, maybe a nightmare or something. Then I heard a female voice answer.

"I knew we didn't have a female in the room, and I could tell, it wasn't your voice at all, but it was a male voice. It sounded as if the voices were centered right in the middle of the room, between the beds and near the bathroom.

"I know I wasn't dreaming. Then the voices got a little bit softer and more mumbled. That made it really hard to understand what who, or whoever it was, was saying.

"About the last thing that I remember, was that it sounded as if the mumbled tones were moving further away from where they first were heard. Just like two people walking away," he said.

"And I missed it all!" I cried out. "You should have woke me up!"

"It did cross my mind, but then I thought, if I say something to wake you up, then the ghosts would disappear for good. That's why I didn't." Kenny responded.

I went ahead and got up and showered and got dressed. I was disappointed. I was glad that Kenny had the ghostly experience of hearing the voices of that couple, but I was sad about missing the entire dialogue. I must have been dead to the world in sleep.

As I was packing, I kept thinking that maybe, it was the 'Lady in Blue' or possibly, could it have been another ghostly visitor of the hotel, trying to enjoy a little Halloween Happenings as well?

Next Halloween, I can reserve this same room and try it again.

I'll Leave You Alone if You Leave Me Alone at the Seelbach Hotel

Prior to each ghost walk, I stroll through the Seelbach Hotel to check things out before bringing guests inside for the last story and stop. On this particular evening, one of the doormen, Jordan asked me if I'd heard the latest ghost story. I told him no, and was eager to hear of the most recent paranormal experience from the hotel.

"It happened this week," Jordan began.

"Nick told me about it, and he said that a guest was upset about the experience. Nick, another one of the doormen, was called to help her with her luggage. It turned out he was the first person she saw that she could tell.

"Nick said that she was real agitated, nervous, and eager to depart from the hotel.

"The lady had something strange, something ghostly that happened in her room."

"Do you know the room or the floor?" I asked Jordan.

"I don't know the exact room number, but it was the 8th floor," he said.

"Jordan, isn't that the floor you heard the voices awhile back?" I asked him.

"Yes, it is, but I wish I knew the room number to this room, and I'm sorry that I don't," Jordan replied.

"The guest told Nick that she was in her room and that the television was turned on. She was in the bathroom getting ready and listening to the television.

"She stepped out from the bathroom and glanced toward the television. For some reason, the television screen went blank. Then, some strange shape appeared on the screen," he said.

"Did she describe the shape to Nick," I asked Jordan.

"Well, she said it was almost like a large, white eye, with a dark dot in the center, and the background remained a deep blue color," Jordan said.

"The lady told Nick, she just stopped in her tracks and stared at the 'big eye' that was in the center of the screen, and she said that it just about gave her the creeps.

"It was almost like some alien or extraterrestrial being was watching her.

"Nick said she told him that she slowly walked over the television and smacked it on the side lightly, thinking it was some malfunction. Next, it just went to a blank screen, blue color.

"The lady said she started thinking about the ghosts that haunt this hotel. She said out loud to the television, 'I'll leave you alone if you leave me alone.'

"At that point, the television went back to the normal screen with the program she was watching."

"The last thing she said to Nick was, 'During the night, something would cause me to wake up. I'd look toward the television, and I know it was just my imagination, but it did look like the 'big eye' had reappeared on the screen. Something was watching me as I slept; but I kept telling myself, "I'll leave you alone if you leave me alone."

It's A Haunted House in New Albany, Indiana

Once you cross the Sherman Minton Bridge, all the motorist has to do is take the first exit into New Albany, Indiana. Follow the signs to the Culbertson Mansion, located at 914 East Main Street, and you'll get to experience one of southern Indiana's true, haunted houses.

William Culbertson was a dry-goods merchant who turned entrepreneur and he had the mansion built for his second wife, Cornelia. The three-story mansion was constructed between 1867 and 1869 and it contains twenty-five rooms. Some of the noteworthy features of the mansion are the marble fireplaces and a carved rosewood staircase. The state of Indiana owns this particular piece of property now as a historic home.

Mr. and Mrs. Culbertson lived in the French styled mansion for many years. Mr. Culbertson had three wives. He was widowed twice, and remarried for the third time at age 70.

The furnishings in the house are not original at all. In fact, the furniture is only period furniture, so none of the Culbertson family members ever used those items that are on display. However, that doesn't dampen any ghostly activity in the residence.

Most believe the ghost that haunts the mansion is his second wife, Cornelia Culbertson. I tend to think otherwise. Cornelia isn't the only ghost that haunts this mansion and I've experienced 'something' to confirm my belief.

I have visited and toured the Culbertson Mansion on several occasions. On each visitation, the purpose was to check the existence of ghosts, and I never left disappointed.

What you're about to read is my accounts of my investigations and experiences at the historic Culbertson Mansion. Maybe you'll get to

Culbertson Mansion.

I was with a group of ghost hunters from the Seattle, Washington, area one August. This group came to Louisville to investigate Waverly. They had contacted me about doing a ghost walk, and asked me about other locations. I recommended the Culbertson Mansion and I was able to make the needed connections for a private tour.

So many people think ghosts become active only at midnight, or on the date of Friday the 13th. And some think that ghosts are only active in the month of October, and the closer to Halloween, the better. Those are all misconceptions and myths.

The group and I were able to investigate the Culbertson Mansion early on a Saturday morning. We were able to explore the mansion from 8 A.M. until 10 A.M. The guide met us there and led us on a historical tour first. It's important to know the background, the history of the house, and family.

As the guide led us throughout the house, she provided us with information about some of the things that have occurred there, all unexplained and mysterious. And some of those things happened to us.

In the nursery on the second floor, we had gathered into the small room. Our attention was directed upon an antique bassinet with a small doll inside.

The guide told us that one of the mysteries of the house is when 'someone' would turn this doll over, leaving it face down in the bassinet. This 'someone' is someone with unseen hands that tend to haunt the house. Nobody, such as guides or curators would touch such an antique artifact of the house and try to play pranks on each other. But why would it happen? And who would turn it upside down?

The guide also told us about the small pantry that was adjacent of the dining room. This room would often smell of flowers, or the heavy fragrance of perfume from some female, maybe Cornelia.

Once our guided tour was complete, we were free to roam about the house. On several occasions, my guests and I had walked through the dining room, passing through this pantry and leading into the kitchen.

Since it was nearing 10 A.M. we were on our final walk in the house. We had gathered our equipment and were exiting the property. We needed to exit via the kitchen door. I pushed open the door that led into the pantry and was almost knocked down with the heavy fragrance of flowers. I said to my guests, "Do you smell what I smell? It's flowers, all in this room, but no flowers are here."

We had all entered this room by this time and took deep breaths, breathing in the fragrance of flowers. Or were we breathing in the lingering scent of perfume from a 'ghost.' Either way, we were excited! Was it Cornelia? Was Cornelia proving her existence?

Just as our guide had told us about one of the ghostly hauntings, we had experienced it for ourselves. Our guide had described it so well to us on the tour, and now, we were able to experience it first hand, completely unexpected. The fragrance was heavy in the air. My guests and I just stood there in disbelief and exchanged glances and nods with each other.

Who was this 'she' who filled this room with the aroma of her perfume? Or who was responsible for the fragrance of the flowers? Was Mrs. Culbertson the 'she' that was in the house?

On another visit to the Culbertson Mansion, this one occurred in October of the following year. The mansion offers a ghost tour during October, and the guests have a guided candlelight tour.

My friends, Mr. and Mrs. Brown, whom I have spoken of before in this book, were with me on this particular night. The lights in the mansion were low and we guests were led from room to room by the light of candles.

Candles burning changed the atmosphere of the house and really set the tone for the stories we were about to hear. Stories are one thing, but witnessing something ghostly is another.

We were on the second floor of the house. The tour led us from room to room. We had stopped by the children's room and observed the furnishings and heard some of the history about the children who lived in the Culbertson home with their parents. The children's room had the bed and some antique toys on display.

The guide led us into other rooms and told us how the Culbertsons used the rooms and what is going on in the rooms today. As we continued in the house, our tour took us back into the children's bedroom so we could exit the back staircase and return to the first floor.

I was walking close to the guide, and Mr. and Mrs. Brown were right behind me. We had entered into the children's bedroom, and the guide stopped suddenly. I stopped quickly and so did the Browns. What got our attention was the bed.

We all gasped and stared at the bed. When we were first in the room, just minutes earlier, the bedspread was all smooth and the room was in perfect condition. This time, the bedspread appeared to have been yanked and pulled.

"It looks like some child, in a temper tantrum, had grabbed the bedspread with his hands and yanked off the bedspread," I said. The bedspread was all wrinkled up, and the fabric pulled forward, as if a young child, had just stood there and pulled off the bedspread.

Was the ghost disturbed with the guests in the house?

But that wasn't all that was disturbed in that bedroom.

The children's toys disturbed by unseen hands.

"Now look over there," I said to everyone in the group. There in the corner, the antique toys, such as the tricycle, and play items, were now turned over!

And what I found to be the most unsettling, was a child's baby cradle, and the doll was turned *upside down!*

The candlelight cast strange shadows in the room. A room, that a moment earlier was a prime example of a bedroom of wealthy children from another time period, was now, in disarray. Was something in the room that wanted to send the message of anger and hostility? Was a spirit annoyed that this group of guests was in the house?

This is speculation, but once our tour was complete, my friends the Browns, the guide and I, were discussing what had happened this evening in the children's bedroom. We reached the conclusion that one of the spirits, maybe Cornelia, or maybe that of a child, was troubled by the actions of some of the guests on the tour. It saddened us greatly, when people tour a historical haunted house and instead of being respectful to those who lives have impacted the house and whose spirits still linger, find it entertaining to laugh, poke, and try to scare each other. On this tour, that was a problem this evening. Several guests thought it would entertaining to try to get a scream out of some of the more giggly guests. Some guests thought they needed to continually whisper and try to over talk the guide, which made it difficult for the guide to speak and for the audience to hear. It's been from my opinion that spirits don't like such disruptive behavior, and this might have been the case here in this house.

On my final tour of the Culbertson Mansion, I had one encounter that I often tell about when guests on my ghost walking tour ask about personal experiences. People like to hear about ghosts and their activities, but they tend to change their minds, or quiver a little bit when they find out about a ghost who actually made contact with them.

My sister and I decided to tour the Culbertson Mansion one October night to participate in the haunted candlelight tour. I knew my sister would enjoy it, since this would be her first time doing such an event. I was careful not to say anything about what might happen or my past experiences.

Our guide, Eileen, had brought us into the master bedroom. As I mentioned earlier in this writing, none of the furniture is authentic to the house, yet it is all period furniture, and not reproductions.

Eileen began her presentation to the group of visitors who were already on edge. "When we come into this room, as caretakers of the house, we put on white gloves and dust the furniture, and smooth out the bedspread. In fact, this bedspread is at least, one hundred years old, but again, the Culbertsons never slept in this bed nor under this bedspread.

"We can tell when someone has been in this room because if you look at the bed, now, the bedspread is all smoothed out. However, when someone ghostly has dropped by, we can see the ruffled bedspread where it looks like someone had been sitting. Also we can see what looks like a handprint, pressed down into the bedspread. The handprint leaves an imprint.

"Nobody on the staff here would play such a prank with the artifacts."

At that point, Eileen directed our attention to something else in the room and she began to talk about the life of the Culbertsons, but that was soon interrupted.

"Look at the bed!" cried out a woman on the tour.

We all turned our attention to the bedspread, and there was a handprint on the bedspread! Some guests on the tour gasped, others

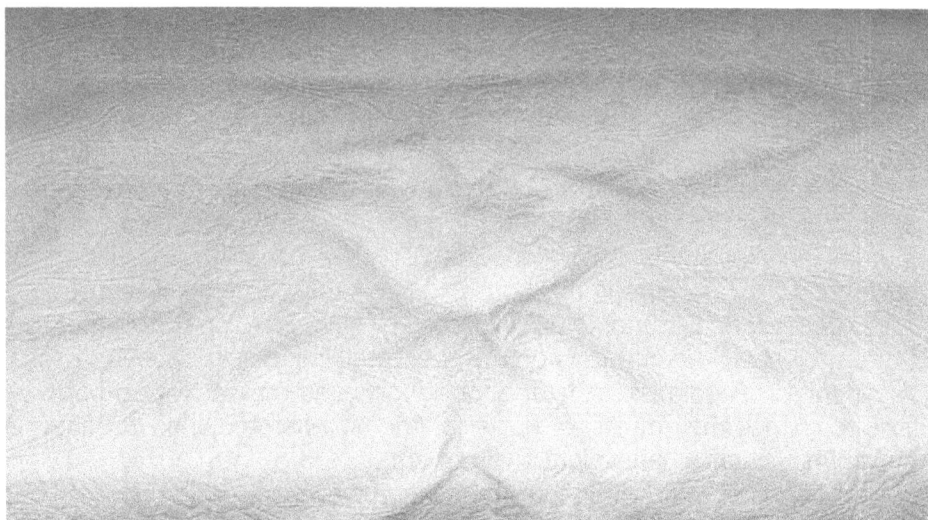

The Ghostly Handprint that appeared!

pointed and some got so unnerved that they even left the room. One by one, the other guests left the room and were talking about what had just happened. That one handprint made a believer out of many of the guests, and that included my sister as well, who had exited the room.

I turned to Eileen, since she and I were the only two left in the room. "Do you mind if I move closer to the bed and take some photographs of the handprint?' I asked.

"No, not at all, go right ahead," and Eileen moved away from the area. "Besides, everyone else has left the room and I'll take them into the ballroom and continue the tour."

I moved closer to the bed and examined the handprint. I dropped to my knees and placed my camera just about eye level with the surface of the bed. As soon as I positioned myself on the floor, I felt two hands on my shoulder. I never paused and looked over my shoulders to see who had hunched over. However, I could feel the fingers and the thumbs on my shoulders. I could feel the strength of the hands bearing down. The hands were not small at all, large, and muscular. But, I never felt any fear or that I was in danger.

I snapped several pictures, and stood up. The only way that I can describe this sensation, is just that feeling of when your arms and legs go to sleep, and the blood circulation returns. I felt this tingling sensation race from my feet, torso, arms, shooting all the way to my shoulders. I felt weak in the knees and I remember holding onto to furniture. As I turned about in the room, I saw nobody present. I staggered into the ballroom, where the guests had gathered.

I noticed a metal folding chair and I dropped into the chair. I recall my head falling backwards, and hitting the wall. My eyes stared at the ceiling. Exhaustion was all I could remember. I could hear Eileen with her presentation, but my body felt weak, and just about limp.

Eileen approached me.

"Robert, are you okay?" she asked.

"Eileen, when you left me in the master bedroom, who else was in the room? Who came over and placed their hands on my shoulders?" I asked.

"Why? Nobody was in the room, Robert. You were alone; besides, I looked back and saw you by the bed," she replied.

"Eileen, someone touched me on the shoulders. I could feel the strong hands, and the fingers, those cold fingers and thumbs," I said to her.

"That had to have been the ghost of Mr. Culberston, Robert! He was a big man, a strong man, and we were in the bedroom that he shared with his wife. I bet that was his ghost, looking over your shoulders and he touched you!" Eileen said.

By then, the others had gathered around me and I told them what I had just experienced. My being touched by a ghost only alarmed them even more, and Eileen pretty much concluded the tour. Her stories wouldn't compare to my being touched by a real ghost!

It still remains a mystery about whose hands made contact with me. I know what I felt. It wasn't my imagination at all. That strange sensation that my body reacted to wasn't my imagination either.

I'd often heard stories from other ghost investigators who had contact with a ghost and told of the same tingling sensation. It's hard to understand unless it happens to you.

But back to Eileen's observation of the hands that touched me. As Eileen observed, maybe it was Mr. Culbertson just being curious about what I was looking at, and he probably wanted to know who I was anyway.

Now I regret not looking over my shoulders to just see if I could see the face of the ghost of Mr. Culbertson there!

Just a Dime's Worth at the Brown Hotel

One of the guests on my tour had a story to tell me about the Brown Hotel. This particular guest was just repeating a story she had heard told from her grandmother.

The Brown Hotel opened in October of 1923. The 13th, 14th, and 15th floors of the building had residential apartment for residents who wanted to live at the Brown. There are no apartments inside of the Brown Hotel today for occupants to call home.

Not many buildings have a 13th floor like the Brown does!

"It had to have been shortly after the Brown Hotel opened and my grandmother, was a young teenaged woman at the time. My grandmother was employed as a housekeeper for some of the residents of the Brown," said my tour guest.

"I don't know for sure if my grandmother was employed by the Brown Hotel as a housekeeper, or had landed this position by applying for the position on her own. Anyway, she tended to this elderly woman's apartment on a regular, almost daily basis doing light housekeeping and running errands and such.

The Brown Hotel's Magic Corner

"Besides this woman being wealthy enough to reside In the Brown Hotel, she paid my grandmother in dimes. And in the 1920s, being paid in cash was normal, and being paid in dimes made the paycheck seem all more special.

"Apparently, my grandmother had formed a unique relationship with this particular woman, so their relationship went beyond just employer and employee.

"One of the stories my grandmother had told me that she was at work one day. The elderly woman was in the apartment. Both of the women heard this loud scream and they both saw something fly past their windows.

"For some unknown reason, a man had gone to the roof and jumped from the side. Those two ladies happened to be in the right spot at the right time, to witness his body pass by their windows and to hear his scream of terror.

"It left an impression upon my grandmother at that time. She often told of being in the apartment and cleaning, and then, something would catch her eye and she would glance toward the window. She spoke of hearing the scream and seeing a body flash past the windows. It was so real looking, my grandmother would often rush to the window and look out, only to see 4th Street below and the usual traffic and pedestrians.

"The particular site and sound occurred with much regularity to the point, that my grandmother avoided being alone in that room of the apartment, or if she did, she purposely closed the draperies over the windows.

"My grandmother reported to work one morning, after being away or off duty for a few days.

"An employee of the hotel stopped my grandmother while she was in the lobby and said to her, 'Would you please come with me; I have some bad news to share with you.'

"Of course, my grandmother feared the worst. Had she done something wrong? Was she being terminated? Going with the Brown Hotel employee, she went into an office.

"The lady you clean for was unfortunately found dead a few days ago. The coroner removed the body. There's no family in the local area to contact, so the apartment is just sitting there, undisturbed. Would you please go into her apartment, and gather up her personal belongings, such as something the body can be dressed in for the funeral, and then, box up the remaining items? Eventually, the apartment will need to be totally cleaned out, and of course, since she was a resident here in the Brown Hotel building, we'll compensate you for your time.'

"My grandmother agreed and went upstairs to the apartment. Upon entering, she felt that the apartment seemed eerily quiet and nothing had been disturbed.

"To my grandmother's amazement, in the secret location where my grandmother would find her payment for her housekeeping services, she saw a stack of dimes.

"My grandmother said that she didn't know whether to take the stack of dimes as she usually did when she was finished, or just leave them. She didn't feel right, taking money from a deceased woman, even though, the stack of dimes was rightfully her money; it was her paycheck.

"My grandmother selected a lovely dress from the woman's closet. She found a hat and gloves, and took the dimes and slipped them into her own purse. With the clothes, hat, and gloves, my grandmother locked the door. She took the clothes down to the office and gave them to the hotel employee.

"The hotel employee asked my grandmother to return in a few days to clean out the apartment and to begin boxing up items.

Historic Brown Hotel Items on Display

"My grandmother arrived a couple days later after the funeral, and went into the apartment. As my grandmother began sorting through the personal belongings and preparing the apartment for the next tenant, my grandmother found a stack of dimes in that secret location that only she and the woman would have known about.

"Grandmother said she just 'froze' standing there, looking at the stack of dimes. Who would have known? And who would have left dimes 'there' since it was their secret location? Was the deceased woman still paying for her services?

"Grandmother took the stack of dimes and deposited them into her purse. Sure, she needed the money. And she continued doing her chores and responsibilities for the hotel and in the memory of the deceased.

"Grandmother returned one final time to help pack everything up and to assist with the moving out of furniture. The employee of the hotel asked my grandmother if there was anything she'd like to have as a keepsake for her to remember the woman by. My grandmother selected a couple small trinkets and dishes, and on the final walk-through of the apartment, my grandmother felt some tugging, some urge, to go look in the secret place of the apartment.

"My grandmother wasn't expecting to find anything there, and just chalked up the last time of finding dimes, just some coincidence, of a fluke.
"But again, to my grandmother's surprise, she found a 'stack of dimes' where the woman would leave payment for my grandmother's services."

Lady in Blue at the Seelbach Makes a Return

At the conclusion of my walks, I tend to linger about the mezzanine level of the Seelbach Hotel chatting with my walkers and getting to know them better. I always take pleasure in hearing their personal ghostly experiences. On this particular fall night in October, 2011, I met two ladies, one who had something to tell me.

The ladies introduced themselves as Jennifer Wilson and Lucy Storms. Neither of the two ladies resided in Jefferson County, but in neighboring counties. They had heard of my ghost walks, and were thrilled to have been on my tour.

The two ladies were very well dressed to have been on a walking tour of downtown Louisville. What I noticed was that both ladies had on heels, attractive jewelry, and fancy scarves tied about their necks.

Jennifer stood tall and slender, with shoulder length dark hair. She had something that she wanted to share with me. Lucy told me she was the skeptic, but she enjoyed the stories. Lucy wasn't quite sure if she wanted to have a ghostly encounter or not.

"Robert, I know you'll understand what I'm about to say. Very few people know this about me that I have this fascination with the hotel's ghost, the Lady in the Blue Dress," said Jennifer, with a childlike grin.

"Can you tell me more?" I asked her.

"If happened about two years ago. I'd always heard about the famed Lady in Blue who haunts the Seelbach Hotel, but I never thought I'd ever have an encounter with her.

"Yes, go on," I encouraged her.

"I'm a believer in ghosts and for some reason, I felt like I had some connection to this mysterious lady. And after hearing your story about the strange knocks on the door when you stayed here at the Seelbach, and what other guests have experiences here, I thought this is something you'd like to know.

"My dinner companion and I had just finished having dinner in the Oak Room Restaurant, here at the Seelbach.

"Prior to coming down here, I decided to wear a blue, taffeta dress for the evening. My companion and I had plans to attend the opera, so we had dinner reservations here first.

"My blue taffeta dress was more on the vintage side than what ladies wear today, but I loved the shade of blue and thought, maybe the mysterious Lady in Blue would appreciate it as well."

I agreed with Jennifer, and commented that I've known people to go on investigations and wear period clothing to have better interactions with the ghosts. So, I never thought her wearing the blue taffeta dress was unusual.

"All during dinner," she continued, "I kept thinking about the Lady in Blue, and wondered, if by any chance, she was in the restaurant, or even haunted any part of the Seelbach Hotel anymore.

"We finished our meal, and my companion and I were exiting the restaurant. He had parked his car in the garage that is behind the hotel. We departed though the lobby and made our way into the back hallway that leads to the garage.

"Since the weather was less than ideal, he asked me to just wait here by the automatic doors and he'd return with the car.

"It seemed like an eternity. I paced up and down the hallway and realized that this was just about as eerily quiet as it could be. I was alone in a deserted hallway area. I glanced out the glass doors and only saw darkness.

"I'm sure this was only my imagination, but as I stood at the exit doors, I looked the length of the corridor. For some reason, I blinked my eyes a time or two, and the hallway appeared to have extended in length. It seems like it just grew in length, but I knew that wasn't possible.

"Hallways just don't extend, right?

"As I just strolled up and down the hallway, I noticed much cooler air. I kept thinking about the Lady in Blue, and wondered, *if she was anywhere near my location, or just haunting the tenth floor?*

"I said to myself, '*Oh, Lady in the Blue dress, if you're here, give me a sign.*'

"Nothing happened. I returned to the door and never saw my ride. I turned about and continued walking the length of the hallway toward the hotel. For some reason, I felt real restless.

"I said to myself again, '*Oh Lady in the Blue dress, if you're here, give me a sign.*'

"All of a sudden, I heard three loud stomps on the ceiling above me. I stopped, looked upward and turned about staring at the ceiling. I couldn't help but think, *Was that my sign?*

"I just assumed, oh, it must be the guests above me, and I just chuckled to myself. I looked toward the doors and noticed that the car was at the entrance. I took off walking quickly and exited the Seelbach.

"During the performance at the opera, I kept wondering, *was that my sign that I'd asked for? Did the Lady in Blue, stomp on the ceiling to let me know she was there and that she appreciated my blue taffeta dress?*"

"Jennifer," I began, "When the Seelbach built the Medallion Ballroom much later, it became an addition. It's not apart of the original structure that was built in 1905. If you'd go outside and looked up toward the roofline of the building, you would have noticed one thing."

Jennifer looked puzzled at me. I could tell that once she exited the building, she got into the car and left the property and never bothered to look around.

"Jennifer, the location where you were standing...has no second floor. It couldn't have been guests on the upper floors since there is no upper floor. I believe you *did* contact the Lady in the Blue dress after all and she decided to make her presence known to you as you waited for your companion...just as she had done decades ago. I do believe she appreciated you wearing the blue taffeta dress, and felt that connection back to you as well. You should feel honored," I said to her.

Late Night Knocks at the Seelbach

It was Halloween weekend, 2010. My friends and I enjoy participating in the Adult Halloween Costume Party that the city of Louisville sponsors downtown at the 4th Street Live complex. On previous years, we'd just attend the party and drive home very late at night. On this particular year, I approached the Seelbach Hotel and asked about reserving two rooms for that Saturday night's event. It would be so much more convenient to have the rooms so we could dress, stay as late as we'd like at the party, and just walk across the street, and return to the hotel. I didn't request any special area of the hotel at all other than just two rooms.

When we arrived on that Saturday afternoon, I went to do the check in process. To my surprise, my reservationist at the hotel was able to reserve two rooms for my party on the 10th floor. I was thrilled. I'd heard plenty of stories of hauntings on the 10th floor and I wanted to spend the night on that floor.

The bellman had our luggage on his cart. When I handed him our room keys with the location, his exact words were, "Nobody else is on the 10th floor tonight. You all can make as much noise as you want to make and nobody will be disturbed."

We departed the elevators and had to make a couple direct turns to reach the Muhammad Ali side of the building. We walked the length of the hallway. This side is significant because it has the original, dark wooden doors, not the fancy, white replacement doors found elsewhere in the Seelbach. We were assigned to rooms 1001 and 1002.

The rooms we had couldn't have been nicer rooms, but it was obvious that these rooms hadn't really been modified too much over the decades. I

Lower Level Staircase at the Seelbach

liked that! The ghost would feel welcome, if she chose to make her presence known.

Since we were the only parties on the floor, we were able to keep our room doors propped open and move back and forth into each other's room as we prepared our costumes. We soon had readied ourselves and away we went to the costume party.

Around midnight, I commented to my companion, Michael Risinger, that I'd had enough of the party atmosphere at 4th Street Live and was ready to return to the hotel. He agreed. We had already lost our friends in the mob and knew we'd see them back at the hotel in the morning.

Michael Risinger and I returned to our room and relaxed a bit. A comment was made for some ice for some night cap drinks. I know a lot about the hotel, but as I said to Mike as we were stretched out across our two beds watching television, I didn't know where the ice machine was located. We'd need to go find it.

We walked down the hallway and turned. We then walked the length of the 4th Street side of the building. As we walked, I filled Michael in on the details of the Lady in the Blue Dress who is known to haunt the 10th floor. We walked all the way and entered into the dark, Grand Ballroom.

The Grand Ballroom was eerie already. Some type of a dinner had been in here. The lights were out, but it was apparent, guests had been in here for the dinner. Place settings were still at the tables. One light shown around the crack of an employee door.

I said, "Come on Mike, I feel almost like an employee here anyway. Follow me."

I pushed open the door and we found ourselves walking the cavernous hallways that eventually, led into a kitchen.

The kitchen employees were just as surprised to see Mike and me, and said, "Look, it's Mr. Ghost Walker, right here in our kitchen! Now, don't go you stirring up any ghosts! It's creepy enough to be up here in this lonesome area on Halloween night."

"Creepy place?" I asked them. "What do you mean? Do you think this area is haunted?" I asked.

One of the workers chimed right in, "Yes, this place is haunted." Another added, "We hear footsteps, noises, sounds, and even voices when we're up here all alone, and there's nobody else around here. Don't you go stirring up those ghosts! Everybody knows this place is haunted."

I told the workers I was only looking for ice at this time. One of them filled the bucket, and Mike and I wished them a good and peaceful night.

Back in our room, we enjoyed a beverage while talking about the ghosts of the hotel. I'd shared with him what I knew about the hotel's history, and the stories of the Lady in the Blue Dress. We turned out our lights around 1:30 A.M.

My bed was positioned just a few feet from the entry door. Michael's bed was opposite, near the western side of the room away from the door. I fell right to sleep and from what I gathered, Michael drifted off to sleep just as quickly.

Knock, knock, knock, on the door, caused me to spring forward from my sleeping position. I stared at the door. The first thing I noticed was that I couldn't see any feet that would break the light from the hallway. I never heard anyone speak, or if it was our friends from across the hall, neither of them called my name. And, if it was our friends, had they returned to their room, I never heard them open or hear their door slam close. I heard nothing. I looked at the alarm clock, and it read, 1:40 A.M. I laid back down and fell back to sleep, thinking very little about what had just happened.

Knock, knock, knock was sounded once again on the door. I sat upright in the bed and stared at the door. Again, I never saw any feet breaking the light, and I never heard one word being spoken from the outside. I thought if it was Jacalyn and Tyson, they would have called my name, or at best, sent me a text to announce their visitation. If it was Jacalyn and Tyson, they silently moved to their room. I looked at the clock and it was now, 2:15 A.M. I laid back down and fell back to sleep, knowing I'd see them in the morning.

In the morning, we all met in the lobby for breakfast. The first words from my mouth to Tyson Long and Jacalyn Norwood were, "Did you come over to our room and knock three times on our door at 1:40?"

Those two looked puzzled by my question and just looked at each other. "No, we were still at the party at 4th Street Live," said Tyson Long.

"Well, I heard three knocks at 1:40 and thought it was you. Did you come and knock on the door at 2:15?" I asked.

Tyson Long and Jacalyn Norwood just looked at each other. "No, it wasn't us. We were in our room by then, and we knew you two would be fast asleep," Tyson Long said.

The words from the doorman kept returning to me. "Nobody else is on the 10th floor and you all can make all the noise you want." If nobody was there, then who knocked on our door?

Was that the Lady in Blue, roaming the 10th floor of this historic hotel, as she did on her fateful night of her death? Is she still seeking her husband?

In October of 2011, I had the opportunity to return to the Seelbach Hotel and stay in the very same room as the year before. History does repeat itself. My friends and I attended the 4th Street Live Adult Halloween party.

As the night unfolded, I had returned to the room around 2:00 A.M. My friend Kenny Dowell came into the room shortly afterwards. We turned out our light around 3:00 A.M. The room, as far as I knew, had only the two of us occupying it during the night, but that was about to change.

The next morning, Kenny Dowell woke up first and roused me from my sleep. He asked me if I heard anything during the night and I said no.

"So, you didn't hear voices or talking?" Kenny said.

"No, I slept pretty sound all night. Did you?"

"I woke up hearing voices in the room. At first, I thought it was you, talking in your sleep.

"I sat up in the bed and looked your way, and I soon realized that talking wasn't you, and nor, was it coming from outside. The voices, which I couldn't really tell, what was being said, were in this room.

"I looked at the clock and it was 4 A.M. As I sat still in the bed, I tried to hear the best I could, but the voices seem to fade from any hearing range.

"When they stopped and I heard nothing else, I laid back down and fell asleep.

"There was something in this room," Kenny Dowell said. "The voices kept on going, until they just became softer and softer, until that was it. I couldn't hear anything else. That's when I just laid back down and fell asleep."

Was the Lady in Blue, making her return visit to the Seelbach Hotel? Did I know she was trying to make her presence known, one more time, and unfortunately I was asleep and Kenny Dowell heard her?

There's a spirit inside of the Seelbach, and whether it is the Lady in Blue, or possibly, some other restless spirit that just remains to be known, at this time, unless she comes a knocking again.

My Great-grandfather's Cane of New Jersey

As the owner of Louisville Ghost Walks, often times I'm asked to do a public speaking engagement. I try to accommodate and put together a program for whoever contacts me for a presentation of the ghosts of Louisville. In October of 2013, I was the guest speaker to the Masonic Homes of Kentucky. It was a pleasant afternoon with the residents of the homes.

After the presentation, I met one of the residents by the name of James Mattingly. Mr. Mattingly lingered about, after the presentation and said that he'd like to share something with me if I had the time. I was more than happy to stay and speak with Mr. Mattingly. From his approach to me, I was curious as to what he had to say.

"I thoroughly enjoyed hearing you speak on ghosts and what you said, brought something to memory for me, and it might be of interest to you," said Mr. Mattingly.

"I have a cane that is haunted, and after listening to you speak, I want to give you the haunted cane."

Now that really sparked my curiosity.

I pulled out a chair and sat down and joined Mr. Mattingly at the round table. "You have a haunted cane? I want to hear more about this," I responded. "How is the cane haunted?"

"It started in 2005, and I was on eBay. One of the listings was for an auction item that sold for $5.00 and it was described as being a *haunted cane.*"

"And you won the bid," I chimed right in.

"Yes, I did, and in fact, I think I was the only bidder. The cane came with a history. The seller's name was Tony De'Angelo and he and I exchanged a couple emails before I even won the auction. I was curious, too, about a

haunted cane, and Tony sent me a statement giving me a little more information.

"This is the description that piqued my interest for the eBay listing. How could I refuse?

"'Wooden cane- possibly haunted with the spirit of great-grandfather" is how Tony listed the item on eBay?"

"Tony, the owner of the cane provided me with this information. Tony's great-grandfather was born in Portugal in 1912. After jumping ship in Newfoundland, he made his way through Canada to America.

"Arriving, or a better way to put it, sneaking into America during the Great Depression, Tony's great-grandfather disguised himself as a priest.

"His great-grandfather says that he 'borrowed' the clothes he used as a priest, and he was able to move about America unnoticed. People respected him as being a man of the cloth.

"Once he got established, my great-grandfather was able to bring over his wife, and he stopped the charade of being a priest. He soon blended into the big melting pot of New York City with the countless other immigrants.

"For some reason, maybe a better life, my great-grandparents crossed the river and they settled in Newark, New Jersey, and started a family there.

"My great-grandfather remained in the New Jersey area and raised his family. My great-grandfather passed away in 2004 while he was trying to get out of the bed, and he was using this cane.

"Tony sent me another email just prior to winning the bid.

"Please help me get rid of this wooden cane," the email from Tony wrote.

'My children believe the cane has the spirit of their great-grandfather, who passed away, while holding the cane. The cane would be hanging on the doorknob, and it would move unexpectedly, startling the children. Sometimes it would get warm to the touch for no reason.

"'We just want the cane to go to a good home,'" was the final email that I got from Tony.

"And now, Mr. Ghost Walker, I'm passing the haunted cane along to you, so you can provide the cane to a good home," said James.

Not Being Alone at Patrick O'Shea's on Main Street

Today, the block bounded by Second Street to the west and First Street to the east on Main Street is known as the Whiskey Row/ Iron Quarter buildings. Life has returned to several of the building on the western end of Main Street, thanks for the opening of the KFC YUM Center in October of 2010. Several restaurant owners had a vision and saw this as a wonderful way to restore some of the neglected and abandoned buildings, and breathe new life into them by opening up food service establishments for patrons.

One such familiar name in the Louisville market of restaurants if that of the O'Shea Family restaurants of Irish food. Founder, Tom O'Shea's of the O'Shea's on Baxter Avenue, his brother Mike O'Shea, and a business partner, decided to venture forward and open a new Irish Public House on Main Street. The building selected at 123 West Main Street was built in 1870, and housed several distilleries over the decades. In

(Left) Entrance to Patrick O'Shea's
(Right) Whiskey barrel stains can still be seen on the floors

the distillery industry, the name Wright and Taylor's Old Charter Distillery occupied that location until it ceased operation in 1935. The next occupant was C. J. Schoch and it became the home to the Schoch Heating and Supply Company until 2006.

In 2006, the O'Shea's Public House signed the deal and restoration began on the beautiful building. The four-story building was redeveloped as a pub and event space location. On the outside, the vertical sign bares the name of the youngest entrepreneur and partner, Tom's son, Patrick O'Shea.

"This is an exciting time," began the young, dark haired, Patrick O'Shea, dressed with a typical black apron folded over his sweatshirt and tied at his waist and Levi jeans on the day of our interview. He invited me to have a seat at the nearest table. I heard the chain from his wallet hit the wooden seat he sat down in. His outstretched legs to reveal his high top Nike sneakers, so he was not the usual restaurant and bar owner. "We opened on February 5, 2010, and life hasn't been the same."

I thanked Patrick for his time and welcoming me into the restaurant that was hustling with bar business and patrons enjoying traditional Irish foods. I was eager for Patrick to provide me with a tour of the building, its history, and ghost stories.

Tables made from original lumber from the building

As we strolled about the length of the restaurant, we passed rows and rows of tables.

"We tried to use as much of the original wood as possible during restoration of the building," Patrick explained.

The tables are made from the lumber from walls that we had to remove and expand. We didn't want to waste any of the natural resources and the goal was to incorporate as much of the original, 1870's building into the interior design as possible.

"The round, dark barrel marks stained the wooden floors from their decades of preservation there. It's quite fitting that distilleries housed liquor here, and now, all these years later, we're serving liquor to our guests at the bar.

"The building has a ground floor that exits out onto Washington Street. We use a couple rooms there as our office space. Our plan is for that to house the band or private events, since it has its own entrance onto Washington Street. I do know that when Schoch had the heating business here, they had large garage doors at the Washington Street end and they just drove their trucks onto the ground level.

"The first floor, which is the front entrance from Main Street, is the main bar and dining room. The ceiling in the main dining room near the front is original to the building. We simply just brushed it up and restored its luster.

"We added the staircase to the second floor and from the third level ceiling, we installed that skylight to give it a more warehouse, natural lighting feel.

"Above us, are two more closed floors that we hope to have available for private parties one day, but for now, we use them as our construction room and for storage."

I asked Patrick if he'd ever experienced anything paranormal while he's been at the building, either alone or with others around. Patrick told me no, but he told me which employees that I would need to speak with, because they have had strange things to occur, and it's probably safe to say, the building is haunted.

On one of my numerous visits to Patrick O'Shea's, two waitresses took me to the upper floors. The elevator doors opened and we were on the third floor. We stepped off the elevator and moved about with the glow of the light from our cell phones. Once the light switch was found, it revealed to us what that building had looked like from decades of abandonment. Large windows were at one end and the wide, rough boards made up the floor. It was the construction, carpentry zone with stacks of old lumber, stain and cans of paint, and tools scattered about. Old furniture, sagging cushioned chairs, and sad faced photographs of forgotten people were left behind, with their dusty frames and cracked glass portraits leaning against the walls. The fourth floor looked similar, one with more construction supplies than the other, but both floors had this in common. They were just shells of the purposes they had once served, from a long ago, forgotten time period of the liquor industry.

Patrick had heard some reports of some ghostly activity on the upper floors from this employee and he wanted me to speak directly to him. After a couple phone calls, I was able to track down my contact.

This employee that I spoke with agreed to meet me off site and not at the Main Street location. He no longer works at that downtown location and he wishes to remain anonymous. This gentleman helped out with the construction part of the building, mostly doing odd jobs, such as carpentry work and staining of the wood. The fourth floor of the building was being used as the construction zone.

According to my contact, he'd report to work early in the morning, some mornings as early as 5 A.M. He'd let himself inside, go upstairs and begin working on whatever needed to sawed, stained, or hammered into place. It was on one of the mornings as he glanced up and looked about, that he realized he wasn't alone. It wasn't another employee, but that of a little girl who was making her presence known to him. She had the white, pale appearance of a ghost, and watched him curiously. He heard nothing, no sounds, and no vocal communication from her or any other apparition from that area on the floor. Within minutes, she had simply faded away.

Another one of my contacts was one of the managers of Patrick O'Shea's. Justin Marcum was there prior to opening day and remained there until his transfer to another O'Shea's Family restaurant in the city almost one year later. Justin had several things to share with me.

I met Justin Marcum for the first time for our interview at Brendan O'Shea's on Shelbyville Road. He joined me at the bar and extended his hand. He positioned himself on a barstool, brushed crumbs from his black pants, smoothed down his necktie, and readjusted his plaid, Irish gentleman's hat. He relaxed a bit, smiled, and began sharing with me some of his experiences.

He was quick to stress one thing to me. "I never considered myself to be a believer in the paranormal, or ghosts, or any of that stuff you hear about, but my opinion changed," said Justin.

"I was never afraid. It wasn't a ghost that wanted to project fear to me or to any of the employees either. I just thought it was a ghost that was glad that people were in the building once again. It had been abandoned for years, and all of sudden, construction workers were here, and plans for the building were coming together.

"Our office at that time was located on the ground floor," he said.

I told Justin I'd been on that level of the building during my tour with Patrick, so I was familiar with the layout.

"I'd be down there late at night and I'd hear the normal footsteps above, creaks, groans, and I'd just dismiss all those sounds as an aging building, that's all. It would sound like someone was walking upstairs on the main floor when I knew, nobody was here and the building was secure. Or, that's how I would reason it out," he said with a smile. "It is easy to be creeped out in a building that old.

"Sometimes, the walking was be intense enough that I'd leave this area and I'd go upstairs to the main floor and investigate. The front door would be locked and just about all the lights would be off. I'd walk the length of the main dining room, past each table, each partition for the booths, and nothing would be found. At the far end, we have a balcony that looks down over Washington Street. With my hands pressed against the glass on the doors, I'd only see my own reflection in the glass doors, as I'd stand there looking down onto the deserted street.

"Back downstairs, I'd feel as if I wasn't alone. Someone was there, and I got used to feeling of 'not being alone' anymore.

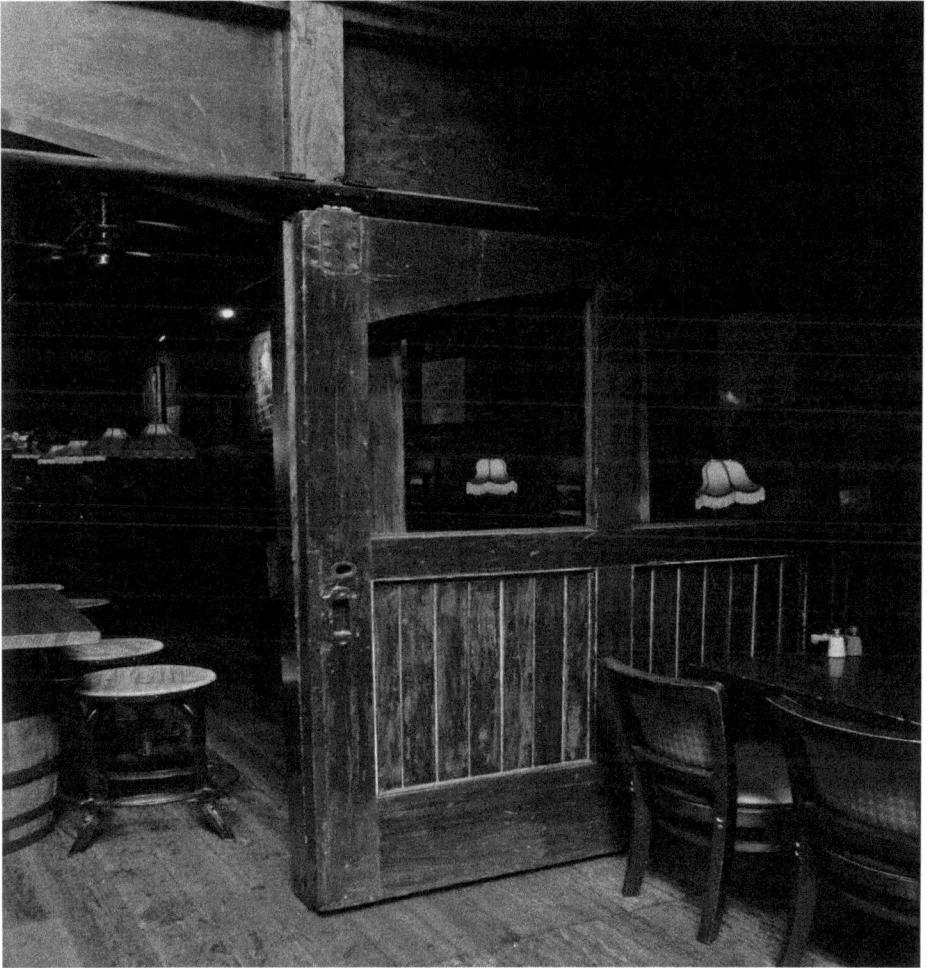

"The security cameras had a red light that would keep going off when it would pick up movement on the upper floors. I'd notice the monitor and something would be moving on the second floor of the building."

"How did it look?" I asked Justin.

"It looked like a man that was walking on the second floor. It appeared to be on the right side of the floor, just like a figure that was walking toward Washington Street. It had the grayish tint. The monitor shows images in black and white, or shades of gray, no real color, but this male figure, he sure did appear gray.

"When we'd leave for the night, the sensation was the strongest. There was the sensation of feeling some 'presence' with me as I was leaving or heading out the door. I wasn't the only one who felt such a presence being with me, or with others. Different ones would comment, and it didn't matter if I was alone or not. Nothing really was scary about it, or strange. It felt a little creepy, but I'd say, whatever it was, was friendly and really didn't mind that we were there. It seemed to enjoy us being there. I got the sensation it was sad that I was leaving for the day.

"The buildings here on Main Street, were vacant so long, I believe, having people in here once again, made whatever it was, a little happier. It brought it back to some life form."

"It liked to interact with you," I commented to Justin.

"Exactly, I believe it," added Justin.

"So there was never any fear?" I asked.

"Oh, it startled me a few times, and would make me more in touch with it as I worked there. I would know, at certain points in time, that its presence was near or around me on the ground floor or up in the building."

"Did you open up the restaurant?" I asked.

"I did. I was there the day we opened and worked two weeks prior to the opening doing the labor and construction."

"So the ghost got used to having you around," I said to Justin.

"I would say so. Now, that I'm at this location (Brendan O'Shea's) and I know this is going to be hard to say and understand, but I miss the feeling as strange as that is."

"You get used to it," I said.

"I got used to it while I was there, just as it was familiar with me. At the end of the night, I knew I wasn't alone. I know that sounds strange.

"I'd make jokes, and say things in front of the wait staff about, '*I don't want to make anyone mad or upset*' and we'd all know who I was referring too.

"I'd just get used to it, I knew it was there. On occasion, I'd get the creeps and sounds would be heard, but random type noises. Nothing frightening was ever reported, things didn't go flying off tables like you hear and see on television and movies.

"Mostly, I just felt like something was behind me on the Main Street level, or on the sub-basement floor. During construction and remodeling, we dug a sub- basement, for the plumbing and keg storage, lockers for employees. That's when I'd feel like that presence would like to make itself known. The sub-basement was there, but we had to dig it out deeper to accommodate everything to bring the building up to restaurant code.

"Like I was saying before, I'd always look over my shoulder when I'd be leaving from the Main Street entrance. There would be some vibe or sensation, I don't know I'd describe it, but there was something there."

"Did you ever have the urge to turn and look back, just to see if anything was really there?" I asked him.

"Oh, I did more than once, just to see. I never saw one thing, nothing visual, other than the images I'd seen on cameras."

"Did alarms go off late at night?" I asked Justin.

"Alarms have gone off before, but not security alarms, but fire alarms. This is what is odd. The fire alarms would be pulled on game days. The fire alarms would sound randomly, on game days when we had a lot of people here enjoying themselves. Now the mystery remains, we've never had problem with pranksters pulling the fire alarms at the other restaurants at all, but now, at his location, it's happened. We have to evacuate the entire restaurant. People are in here having fun, and this really interrupts what's going on.

"Whatever it is that's hanging around Patrick O'Shea's, is most welcoming. We can only hope, that it is of Irish descent and enjoys a good time," concluded Justin.

Not-So- Magical Corner for the Heyburn Building

When custodian, Nathaniel Carter, was outside cleaning at the Louisville Free Public Library on the morning of Thursday, January 21, 2010, he wasn't expecting what was getting ready to happen. The flash that caught his eye, wasn't a flash of lightning or some flash of electricity, but the flash that caught his eye was that of a man, Tony Ellis, jumping to his death from the eastern side of the Heyburn Building's top floor.

The Courier-Journal newspaper reported that at 10:20 a.m. 39 year old Tony Ellis went to the 17th floor of the Heyburn Building, raised an end window in an alcove hallway, and jumped to his death. As Tony was descending, his body struck part of the second floor's overhang portion of the building before hitting the pavement.

Who Tony Ellis was remains a mystery. He didn't work in any offices of the Heyburn Building and employees who witnessed the fall or saw him prior to the time in the building didn't know him.

Why Tony Ellis selected this historic, 17-story building also remains a mystery. The Heyburn Building, which occupied the site of the former Avery Mansion at the corner of 4th and Broadway, was constructed in 1928. The 4th and Broadway corner was soon designated as the 'Magic Corner' for the growth of retail and commerce, that had just now crossed south of Broadway.

Employees of the Heyburn Building have spoken of the ghost of Tony Ellis that is haunting the building. Office workers who have windows and views looking east have reported to seeing that flash of light, something, seen falling from the window, just as Nathaniel Carter had seen. But the most troubling thing was the ghost that Tony Ellis had seen on the 17th floor.

Security cameras have picked up an image of a man moving down the hallway and stopping at the window. Workers have spoken of seeing a man, pale in color in the hallway on the 17-floor, which appears to be really going nowhere in particular, just a ghostly image.

The most troubling part of it all would be history repeating itself. The ghost of Tony Ellis' activity is more prevalent near and on the anniversary date of January 21.

"I was here at work, that day that Tony jumped to his death," explained one worker who was on the 17th floor.

"I remember seeing him, but really thought nothing else of it. Next thing I knew, word spread throughout the building that a man had jumped to his death! It was hard to believe, but it happened.

"Even though only a couple of years have passed, his ghost still comes back, year after year. Strange things happen around that date in my office, such as sounds of screams, cries, and once, the clock had stopped just at 10:20 one day on the anniversary of Tony's death.

"His ghost is still here, replaying the events of Tony's final day in this building,"

It still remains a mystery as to who Tony Ellis was and why he chose the Heyburn Building. Only Tony Ellis can answer those questions, so we may never know why he continues that deathly ritual.

Oak Room in the Seelbach Hotel

On warm summer evenings, I often sit in the anteroom, just outside the entrance to the famed Oak Room Restaurant, located on the mezzanine level of the Seelbach Hotel. I sometimes make small talk with the bartender, or a member of the wait staff. They see my Louisville Ghost Walk shirt and just strike up a conversation. This night was no different.

The Oak Room wasn't always a restaurant, and it took years before it earned the five-star status that it holds today. When the Seelbach expanded in 1907, the room was at first, the billiards room. The pool stick racks are still on the wall. The columns are adorned with detailed woodcarvings with timeless labor. The room has a natural, masculine feel, so with its touch of masculinity, maybe that explains why one ghost appears to be that of a male.

Jenny Swank was the first to begin conversation with me. I moved from my seated position on the couch and joined her at the bar. Jenny commented about the 'ghosts' of the Seelbach and asked what stories I told my guests.

"I've been working here for a couple years, and nothing had ever happened until one night," she said.

That got my interest and I encouraged her to tell me more.

"It would be easier if I just showed you," she said as she stood up and left the bar. She invited me to follow her into the dining room.

We passed through the main dining room and entered into a smaller room, adjacent to the main dining room. Inside this room, three walls contained all the wine bottles. One wall had a large mirror. In the center was a table for two, complete with the linen tablecloth and the signature china. On the table was a small, silver mint julep cup with fresh red roses.

"Guests can reserve this wine room, and we prepare it for those special occasions. We keep our wine in here and guests can have a memorable dinner in an unforgettable location.

"One night I was getting ready for work. I felt rushed, so I stepped into this room and stood in front of this mirror. I was just fluffing my hair and checking out my clothing attire before heading out onto the floor.

"Another server, rushed into the room and said to me, 'Okay, where did the man go?' I said, 'What man?'

"I saw a man standing in here, just right behind you. Where is he?' she demanded to know. She had jumped to conclusions that I had a man hidden in the wine room, and she even looked around! Of course, there was no man to be found.

"I asked her to describe this so-called man she had seen.

"She said he was taller than me, standing right behind me. All she could say was he was dark, or shadowy, which she blamed on the lighting inside this room.

"I don't know if I was ever able to convince her that I had no man in this room."

We walked back into the dining room and I asked Jenny if she could show me where the other server was standing when she saw the apparition. We hadn't moved far from the doorway at all. We stood just beyond a table and for the most part, we had an unobstructed view right into the wine room. Whatever the other server saw, clearly made an impression that she thought a human being was standing behind Jenny.

"But that's not the only ghost story," she said as we walked toward the main entrance. "Just a short while back, a couple was enjoying their meal. They were seated at a table by the window.

"I didn't find this out until after they finished dessert, and come to find out, they both saw something, but remained quiet. They didn't want the other person, to think they were 'crazy' or imagining things.

"I was told by the couple, that as they were enjoying dinner, something caught their eye. First, they noticed the chandelier that was starting to sway back and forth. Neither said a word, but watched the chandelier.

"Next, at different times, a white fog, or mist, would appear over in this corner, which is opposite of where they were seated. Again, neither commented to the other, but they were both observing whatever it was.

"These strange, ghostly behaviors continued right into dessert. Finally, one of them commented to the other, 'I've been watching the chandelier sway and the funniest thing, something white, almost like a fog would appear near that table and rise upwards.'

"And he said back, 'You too!' I've been watching it as well, but didn't want to say anything, thinking it was my imagination!'

"That's when I found out about it. I was either serving dessert, or clearing away their dishes, and they both told me about it. I turned and looked in that corner, but at the time, I didn't see the chandelier move nor did I see any thing that appeared to be a white substance or fog.

"That couple saw something, they were both positive about it. It's funny how people will just watch and wonder, without saying anything when they are in the presence of something ghostly."

"I don't think it was anything that would harm or frighten your diners," I commented to Jenny. "With the hotel being over 100 years old, and the history of this particular room, there's really no telling who or what could be haunted this dining room today."

Returning Ghosts of Room 1001

Each Halloween weekend, I have this tradition of spending the night at the Seelbach Hotel in downtown Louisville. For one, it's a great reason to stay at this historic hotel; but for another reason, I do several downtown Halloween events that includes the hosting of Louisville Ghost Walk Tours and other festive parties, so it makes sense to just 'stay the night.' Halloween of 2013 was no exception.

I made my reservation in advance to secure my personal room, as I like to call it up on the 10th floor.

Most of the employees of the hotel know me. They know that I bring many guests into the hotel as part of my business of Louisville Ghost Walks. Upon checking into the hotel on the Saturday afternoon I engaged Michael Yanovich, the night desk clerk who was working, in some conversation.

Michael Yanovich has been with the hotel for a couple of years and plans to go into hotel management. He is always dressed well, to reflect the professionalism of the hotel's staff, with his dark suit, white suit, and traditional striped necktie.

Michael Yanovich is a believer in ghosts. During the check-in process, he shared with me his personal take on ghosts and his own experiences.

"I'm a believer in ghosts, and I'd love to have some kind of a experience down here. The only thing that I've witnessed here is that on occasion, the door to this glass bookcase door will open."

Michael Yanovich turned and opened the glass door that was just behind him. He wanted to show me what he was talking about. "It will just swing open, yet, it's got a lock; something has to unlock it before it will open," he said.

"I think something is just wanting to get your attention, Michael, and nothing else," I told him.

I asked Michael as we finished up the check-in process, "What is the occupancy for the hotel tonight?"

"The hotel has about 50% occupancy for tonight," he said.

"So, depending on how you look at things, it could be half full of guests, or half empty," I replied back.

Leading up to my next question, I asked, "And how's the occupancy rate on the 10th floor where I like to stay?"

"Just the way you like it, Mr. Parker. You're the only guest upon that floor for the night," Michael said.

That's just what I wanted to hear!

Once I had checked in and received the key, I made my way up to the room to get all settled and prepare for the evening's tour.

Nothing had changed in the room. Everything was just as I had remembered it being from last year, and the year before that, almost like returning home after being away.

After the ghost walking tour, the plan was to attend the Halloween party at 4th Street Live and enjoy the presentation of the other costumes and food. I had invited a companion to join me, so she and I had a big night planned.

Once all was said and done at the 4th Street Live adult costume party, it was near 1 a.m. when party-goers started to bid farewell for the night or head to other locations to continue the parties. We decided to return to the Seelbach Hotel and wrap things up for our night of merrymaking.

It was near 2 a.m. when the lights in my room finally were turned out. I know I hadn't been asleep too long, when I woke to what sounded like a door that had been slammed shut! Not in a neighboring room, but from within my own room did the sound originate from.

I opened my eyes and sat straight up in the bed. Of course, the room was dark, but enough light was in the room to where I could make out the furniture and the placement of things.

The slam was so I loud, it sounded like it occurred right in the room, I thought.

I reached from my bed and turned on the lamp on the nightstand. Nothing appeared to be disturbed in any way. I could see my crumpled costume draped across the other bed just as I had laid it. Near the entryway to the bathroom, were my black high top Chuck Taylor shoes, just as I had left them when I unlaced them and tossed them aside. But the closet door was half open, oh, maybe five to ten inches, but open none the less.

What puzzled me the most was the closet door half open. I don't recall opening the door for any reason, yet it was open. Thinking about the slam, I realized that the door was open, just enough that had someone or something slammed it hard, it would have banged against the door jam and the force, would have caused it to swing back open. Could that have been the case for the closet in my room?

Could some ghostly visitor have decided to drop by my room and announce its presence by slamming a door? Did something decide at that early hour, to come out of the closet?

Since I'd experienced ghostly activity in the room on previous stays, I didn't really ponder the issue much longer. I reached over and turned out the light and returned to my sleep.

However, that wasn't my last visitation of the night.

Between the hour of 3 and 4 a.m., someone else decided to return to my room. I'd heard this before. Voices this time had returned as like last year. In my room, were my ghostly visitors of some by-gone era, the two voices of a male and female in the room having a conversation. The talking woke me from my sleep and I just laid there in the dark room, with my eyes open trying to figure out what was being said.

Two voices were heard which meant a conversation was in progress in the room.

It sounded as if a male voice was speaking first, and then a female voice responded. The voices were soft, not loud, boisterous, or confrontational so I ruled out a disagreement. Since the two voices were a repeat experience from last year, I just lay in the bed listening. It wasn't possible to understand exactly what was being said, but it was two voices there in the center of the room. The voices grew softer and fainter until it was just a muffled sound, and then they were gone.

Unfortunately, I have no idea who or what those voices were saying distinctly, and I have no clue as to the conversation those two were having.

However, knowing the hotel's history and folklore, as well as the talk among the hotel staff, it there was definitely some presence in my guestroom.

Now, as a reader of this story, I'm sure you're thinking to yourself, that the voices were two other guests in the hotel who happened to be standing in the hallway having a conversation. But I'd like to leave you with this closing thought.

But keeping with Michael's audit report of hotel occupancy, either 50% full or 50% empty. It all depends on your point of view. I'm going with 50% empty, deserted, and vacant, with the exception of a few, nightly visitors who happened to be haunting the 10th floor of the hotel.

Now, the slamming door is another manifestation that on another occasion, maybe revealed in more detail on the next night's stay.

Spirits in the Seelbach Bar

Louisville Ghost Walks offers its guests an optional tour, titled "Spirits and Spirits." The guests hear the stories, but stop along the route and enjoy adult beverages at three restaurants. The tour concludes at the Seelbach Hotel's Bourbon Bar, just adjacent from the main lobby. On this particular night, one of the long-term bartenders, Cindy Starks, joined my group. When she saw me come inside, she welcomed my party and told them about the featured drink, the Seelbach Cocktail, which consists of champagne, Blue Moon beer, served up in a fluted champagne glass and a orange wedge.

Cindy Starks pulled up a stool and brushed back her blonde hair. She began to share one of her ghostly encounters with my guests.

"We had just closed and I was alone in the bar. I was just putting things away and cleaning up behind the bar. I knew all the doors were locked, and that included the lobby doors.

"The jazz band that plays here on Friday nights had already left and those guys had all said their good byes to me. I was alone.

"My back was turned away from the tables and the stage at the far end of the room "I heard, 'Cindy, Cindy,' so I turned about quickly, and saw nobody. I just thought, *I'm hearing things, nobody is here.*

"I went about my chores and closing down the bar, and sure enough, I heard it again, this time, a little bit louder. '*Cindy, Cindy,*' and I quickly turned about, thinking somebody was here in the bar.

"I turned about, and this time, I walked from around the bar, and into the area. I walked the full length, all the way to where the members of the jazz band plays, thinking, that someone was hiding in here, and playing a prank on me.

98

"There was nobody in the bar, but I heard, my name being called, just as plain as day, as if someone was in here."

I asked Cindy if it sounded like it was coming from a man or a woman. She said it definitely was a man's voice who called her name.

Could the voice have been one of the Seelbach brothers Louis and Otto, making their presence known to Cindy? Where one of the Seelbach brothers giving Cindy a little word of encouragement? Cindy can only hope so.

Startling Presence at the Seelbach Hotel

My tour concludes on the mezzanine level of the Seelbach Hotel. My guests are in awe of the marble columns and white marble flooring that has since graced the hotel from 1905. Their eyes are drawn to the sepia toned murals in the lobby that depict Kentucky history. Guests don't always know where to look upon first entering the Seelbach Hotel, possibly at the scroll work adoring the ceiling or the brass colored intricate patterns that make up the balcony railing. But, I caution guests not to over look the presence of any ghosts that might be making their presence known in the hotel.

I had just finished my final narration of the night, detailing the activity of the famed 'Lady in Blue' who haunted the 10th floor of the hotel. As I was shaking hands with my departing guests, four ladies, who had been walking with me, rushed up to me.

Their excitement was contagious. "We've seen her!" exclaimed one of the four women.

I stopped what I was doing, and looked at all four of the ladies, in disbelief as to what I was hearing.

"We've seen her," said another.

By now, those four ladies had my full attention. The only words I could muster out of my mouth were, "Tell me about it!"

One of the ladies began, "The company we work for here in Louisville had a convention, and the Seelbach Hotel was the headquarter hotel. We had rooms on the 10th floor of the hotel.

"We just rode up on the elevator, and we were just talking about the day's events.

"The doors to the elevator opened and we stepped just into the hallway."

History Wooden Chairs at the Seelbach Hotel

"We hadn't gone far," interjected another lady.

"We'd taken a few steps and were in the hallway, when someone said, "Did you see what I just saw?"

"You mean that pale, ghostly looking woman in the blue dress, standing by the elevator?" another said.

"You saw her, and I saw her," and all four ladies were in agreement about what they saw.

"We turned around and rushed back to the elevator area, and she was gone. We just stood there, talking about that woman, and how pale, and white, and the old style, blue dress, but where was she? We never heard the elevator doors open, and we know, she sure didn't go out the window.

"Nothing would do, but we got onto the next elevator car and rode down to the main lobby. We approached the desk clerk, and said, 'Please don't think we're crazy, but, we rode up to the 10th floor and just got off the elevator, and right there, we saw this pale, white looking ghostly lady in a blue dress. Then, we went back, and she was gone! We all saw her!

"The desk clerk, he just nodded in agreement. 'You just saw, our resident ghost,' he said. "And he continued with her sad story, of suicide, or homicide, on her wedding day, by jumping or being pushed, down the elevator shaft. Nobody knows for sure, how she met her death, but her ghost, is still haunting the 10th floor."

Now we know, according to the hotel's history, that this poor, unfortunate woman haunts the 10th floor. She likes to make her presence known by knocking on doors or rattling doorknobs to the guestrooms located on this floor.

She has made her presence known in other areas as well, besides the 10th floor and by the elevator area.

A waiter named Anthony from the Oak Room Restaurant told me that one night he was working in the dining room. The restaurant had closed for the business day and he was alone. He glanced up, and he saw the Lady in the Blue Dress, and she appeared near the back wall of the restaurant. She glided across the floor, reached the other side of the room, and then, she turned, and glided back to where she came from. As she glided across the floor and neared her original point of where she first manifested, she faded from sight.

On another occasion, I met a waiter named James, and he had a story to share with me. James told me that he has worked in the Oak Room for about 15 years, and during the course of employment, he hadn't seen her personally, but he was acquainted with two chefs who had. James continued by telling me that two chefs saw the Lady in the Blue Dress back in the kitchen. Now, neither of the two chefs was working on the same day, but on two separate occasions, she appeared in the kitchen and shook up those two men. Both chefs walked off the job, exclaiming they weren't working in a haunted kitchen. James is still employed with the Oak Room, and he isn't looking forward to having his own personal experience. He did add that he has spoken with guests who have inquired about the famous ghost, or during conversation, shared with him about strange, unexplained events occurring in their rooms.

Peter, one of the front desk clerks shared with me about an experience that two guests had, concerning their encounter with a ghost. He was working the 3rd shift, and a couple hurried off the elevator with luggage in hand, and rushed to the desk.

"I've been a Baptist preacher for years," the man began, "and my wife and I have never seen a ghost! We're not staying here tonight. We are checking out."

Peter asked what was going on, and offered the distraught and visibly shaken couple another room in the hotel. Once the minister and his wife calmed down, they were able to relate the story of the ghost who paid them a visit.

"She just appeared in our room," said the wife. "It was a ghost, she had on this blue colored dress, and she just appeared in our room. We were both wide-awake at the time, and she was standing at the foot of our bed.

"We're just not staying in a haunted hotel," said the minister.

At that point, I just prepared their check out papers and the couple left the hotel.

Now, I always enjoy when I can share any personal experience, no matter how large or small. Ghosts don't always have to make their presence known in mighty ways, but sometimes, in subtle gestures.

The month was October of 2010, and some friends and I were looking forward to enjoying the Halloween events the city of Louisville had planned. We were able to secure two rooms at the Seelbach Hotel. Without asking for any special requests, our reservation clerk had secured rooms for our party on the 10th floor, along the Muhammad Ali Blvd. Side.

The hallway of six rooms was deadly silent as the doorman, who was showing us to our rooms, escorted us. We had two of the six rooms, and no other guests had occupied the neighboring rooms. We had the hallway to ourselves and could travel from room to room.

The room that my roommate Mike and I shared was on the south side, on the corner, while our traveling companions, had a room on the north side, the Muhammad Ali Blvd. side. Their room was located in the middle of the hallway.

We had enjoyed our evening out, taking in all the costumed characters and the music from the 4th Street Live complex. The hour was late, around 12:30 AM when we decided to retire to our rooms. During the course of the festivities, we had separated from our friends and called it a night.

Mike and I prepared ourselves for sleep, and had occupied our beds. My bed was opposite the door to the room and Mike's bed was further away, near the corner of the room. Around 1:30 AM, we turned out all lights and closed the shades. Our room was dark, with the exception of the hallway light that I could see shining from under the door.

As I lay in the bed, trying to fall asleep, I woke to the sound for four distinct knocks on the door. I rose up in the bed, propping myself up on my elbows. I stared at the door, just wondering, who could be knocking on the door. I couldn't see the shadow of any feet standing at the door. I glanced over to Mike, who was asleep. I listened, in case it was one of our friends knocking on our door, and nothing was heard. What puzzled me was that if it was one of our friends, being as high tech, they would have sent a text message first, and not, just came knocking. Since I never saw any shadows of feet, I laid back down. I fell asleep, but my sleep didn't last long. I woke up to the sound of four more, distinct knocks on the door. This time, I sat upright in the bed and just stared at the door. Again, I saw no feet shadows against the door, and heard no movement from the hallway.

When morning came, I asked my friend Mike if he'd heard any such knocks on the room. Unfortunately, Mike said he'd slept through any such knocks on the door. Next on my list, was to inquire of my friends, if for some reason, any one of them came knocking on our door in the early hours of the morning. As I tried to question and reason it out, the response was no, since they hadn't returned to the hotel between 1:30 and 2:00 AM, and by the time the second knock was sounded later in the night, they were fast asleep in their own room. So, with that information, I ruled out my companions.

My first thought was 'Is this the ghost of the famed, 'Lady in the Blue Dress' that I'd heard about, who roams the 10th floor and knocks on the guests' door? Did she, come paying a visit on our door while searching for her husband?

There It Goes Again, at the Seelbach Hotel

On one of my walks in the fall of 2012, I had the opportunity to have a conversation with two of my guests during one of my presentations. I do enjoy interacting with my guests and hearing their stories or watching their reactions to mine, but this dialogue almost stopped me in my tracks.

The last stop on the walking tour is the mezzanine level of the Seelbach Hotel. The guests have a place to sit down and rest, while listing to the presentation, as well as taking in the ambiance of the historic and haunted hotel.

I had just finished the story about the famed 'Lady in Blue' roaming the 10th floor hallway, knocking on guests' doors and rattling the doorknobs.

A wife was seated at the end of the brown couch and her husband was seated in the green and brown striped wingback chair. What caught my eye was that the wife reached over and smacked her husband across the leg. That got his attention and mine as well. I stopped speaking and looked at those two.

She pointed her finger at her husband. In a clear and loud voice, she had something she wanted to say to him and she didn't care who heard it.

"See, did you hear what he just said about the knocks on the door? And you thought I was hearing things?" she said to her husband.

I stopped my presentation and turned to face the couple. I asked, "Is there something you'd like to share with the group?"

"Yes, I do," she began. "We are guests of the hotel. We checked in last night, so that was our first night here.

"We were in the room when I heard four knocks on the door.

"I walked to the door and opened it. Nobody was there. I said to my husband, 'That's funny, nobody's there.'

"And he said to me, 'That's because you're hearing things; now go sit down.'

"Well, a few minutes later, I heard some more knocks. I said to him, 'There it goes again! Somebody's at the door.'

"So I got up and opened the door, and nobody was there! I said to my husband, 'It happened again, surely you heard it?"

"And he said to me, 'You're hearing things again; now go sit down.'"

At that moment, she sat up on the edge of the couch, and said to her husband, "I told you there were knocks on the door... and you didn't believe me."

I looked at the couple and asked, "Do you mind telling us what floor you all are staying on?"

Those two looked at each other, and her husband's face just lost all of his color. They turned to face me and said, "We have a room on the 10th floor!"

I exclaimed to the crowd, "There you go folks; you're hearing about the ghostly knocks on the hotel room doors from actual guests who have experienced the knocks. It happens more often than what people realize."

Two's Company, Three's a Crowd for a Ghost at the Seelbach Hotel

There's a spirit inside of the Seelbach Hotel, and whether it is the Lady in Blue, or possibly some other restless spirit that just remains to be known at this time, unless she comes a knocking again.

Mike Young, one of the nighttime reservation clerks shared this account with me prior to one of my walks. I often ask the employees when I see them and if they are available, if they have heard of any reports of ghostly activity with the walls of the century old hotel. This is what Mike Young told me, back in October of 2011.

"Some ladies were staying at the hotel for the celebration of a bridal party. The ladies had rooms along one corridor of the hotel so everyone could be close together.

"The bride and one of her bridesmaids shared a room. The two ladies were preparing to go out for the evening, and one of them suggested that they take a picture.

"The two ladies decided to set the camera up and program the timer so they could do a group portrait.

"One of ladies set the camera on the dresser, and they positioned themselves on the bed. The camera flashed.

"The two ladies got up and grouped about the camera. They pressed the review button to check out their smiling faces and attractive dresses.

"Not only did they see their own smiling faces, but behind the bride, was another guest, one not of this world, but a pale, ghostly figure who decided to get into the snapshot as well.

"I asked them what exactly did they see? The ladies said it looked like a large, white face was just behind the bride's head. The ladies said, after that face, they could make out the eyes and a mouth, but no other features.

"Curious about what they had on their camera, they got back onto the bed to try to take a second picture in an attempt to recreate it. In this picture, there were only the two ladies in the review screen of the camera.

"Apparently, this ghostly presence only needed to make her appearance just once."

Unpleasant Dreams at the Brown Hotel

It's not uncommon for guests of the Brown Hotel to purchase my books and contact me, or walk with me and contact me later, or just, pick up one of my business brochures in the lobby and contact me. The one thing that is common is that most of the contact, whether it is by phone or E-mail, all starts out the same way.

"I believe my room was haunted," and they'll begin to tell me the story.

During the summer of 2009, I received an E-mail from a woman, who asked me directly in the E-mail, if the Brown Hotel had ghosts of children haunting the guests' rooms. I read her E-mail in great interest, since I'd not heard of any 'ghost children' haunting the historic hotel.

Her E-mail stated, "My husband and I, and two children were vacationing in Louisville. We had a suite on the 12th floor of the hotel. The accommodations were wonderful, and we felt very much at home during our stay.

"One night, I woke up to the sounds of children laughing, and horseplaying in the next bedroom.

"I thought, my children are awake and are jumping on the beds and laughing. I could clearly hear laughing into my room.

"I didn't wake my husband, so I left our room and walked to the room my children were supposed to be sleeping. I opened the door, and my two children were fast asleep, or at least they appeared to be fast asleep, in their bed. I didn't hear a sound.

"At first, I assumed the children heard me coming, ducked under the covers and pretended to be asleep. I stood there, just waiting for a giggle or

The Brown Hotel

or some movement to prove that they weren't asleep.

"The movement or giggling never came from the slumbering children, so I just backed out of the room and returned to my bed.

"I laid back down and dozed off to sleep. A short time later, I woke again to the sounds of children laughing and roughhousing. Immediately, I left my bed and charged toward the bedroom. I swung open the door, only to find both children lying in the same position with their eyes closed tightly, and the sound of their breathing only heard.

"It was at that point, that I started thinking about the possibility of ghosts. It was obvious, something woke me on two occasions with such sounds that children would make, but upon my investigation, nothing was found to confirm.

"This time, I left the bedroom door wide open. I returned to my room, but I never really fell asleep. I just lay there, thinking about ghosts, and if so, why were they haunting the Brown Hotel. And the biggest mystery, children?"

I read her E-mail with great interest, but unfortunately, I wasn't able to shed much light upon her inquiry of the ghost children. That is, until later.

As the summer progressed, I hosted a private event that included guests who considered themselves to be sensitive, and able to communicate with ghosts. I had just finished my presentation to this group of ladies. One of the guests, asked if they could go inside the hotel and look at the lobby. That was an easy request, so we entered the hotel.

Just inside the main foyer and past the doormen, this one lady said, and "What do you know about the children haunting this hotel?"

I stopped and looked at her, and replied, "I only have one account of children, and they are on the 12th floor, not the foyer. What are you thinking?" I asked.

She walked about the foyer, looked at the two grates of former fireplaces, near the doors, and returned to me. "Children, young children have warmed themselves by this fireplace. I'm picking up children were once here in history."

Suddenly, her countenance turned to sadness. She ran her hand over the grate. She moved in closer, almost placing her head against the grate. Next, she turned and looked at me and said, "And one of them died here."

Now, it is pure speculation that the ghostly children heard on the 12th floor are connected to the ghostly presence of children in the lobby. Were the children guests of the hotel with the parents? And for some, unknown reason did tragedy fall to one of the children with a fire? We're still waiting for the answer.

As I mentioned at the beginning of this chapter, guests do contact me. In January, of 2010, I received an E-mail from a woman who stayed here. She made the same statement, "I believe my room was haunted!"

Her E-mail began, "My daughter had to come to Louisville on business, and she was scared to stay at the Brown Hotel. She persuaded me to join her on this two-day trip. My daughter had seen too many of those cable shows that feature haunted hotels, and she just knew, she couldn't stay here with the ghosts.

"We arrived late in the evening and were assigned a room on the 6th floor. The room was lovely, nicely appointed with period looking furniture, spacious and nothing that would imply the room to be haunted. We had room service delivered to the room and prepared for bed.

"My daughter selected the bed she wanted to sleep in, and I occupied the other.

"During the night, I was slapped across the right side of my face. I woke up immediately, sat upright in my bed, and reached up and rubbed my face. I could feel a sting. My first thought was, 'we've been talking about too many ghosts, and boy, did I have a nightmare!'

"I glanced over at my daughter, and she was sound asleep. I looked about the room, still in disbelief, expecting to see a dark shadow or something like that, as how ghosts are portrayed on television. I just dismissed it and choked it up as a nightmare.

"I lay back down, closed my eyes and fell asleep. Within a short time, I was slapped a second time, on the right side of my face. I bolted upright in the bed, looked about the room, stared down at my own hand, and realized, that I didn't reach up and slap myself.

"Something slapped me not once, but twice. My heart was beginning to race. I could feel a sting again, and I knew something was in this room, but what was it?

"I calmed down, and never considered going back to sleep. I sat up in the bed, and just pulled up the white bedspread up near my shoulders. I never lay back down and I just waited until the sun came up.

"I knew I couldn't say a word to my daughter about this slapping incident. I would have to stay mum she was already scared of ghosts and this would only make it worse.

"We went about our business. I must admit, I wasn't looking forward to returning to this room. In fact, I tried to stall as much as possible. My mind kept thinking, 'would we find our things tossed about? Chairs turned over?' Too much television, I thought.

"When we returned, our room looked fine. Nothing was disturbed; nothing was out of order.

"I must admit, I wasn't looking forward to going to sleep. But, darkness soon fell and the hour approached. My daughter got into her bed and drifted off the sleep. Keeping this incident from my daughter, I simply got into the bed, and got back into the same position of sitting upright, with the white bedspread pulled up close to my shoulders. I don't think I ever, fell asleep. All my senses were working overtime. For each noise, creak, groan, or shadow, it would get my attention.

"The sun finally came up. We gathered our things and checked out of the hotel. I never said anything to the desk clerk, who inquired about my stay."

Now, upon receiving her E-mail, I asked the writer some general questions about her belief in the paranormal. Her belief in the paranormal was very general, almost non-existent, skeptic, at best. She wasn't able to give me too many thoughts, other than she was slapped twice on the right side of her face.

I received her E-mail in January, and I wanted to get inside this room and do some more research, if at all possible. I was able to make it happen.

Being January, I knew I'd need to do something special for my girlfriend for Valentine's weekend. I've always been on a positive relationship with the Brown Hotel, so I went to the hotel and I was able, to reserve this room. I had the haunted room reserved for Saturday, February 13 and 14, 2010.

My girlfriend and I arrived on the afternoon of the 13th. We were both excited about the possibility of lodging in a haunted room.

Just as the writer described, it was a great room, with all the amenities one would expect from a hotel of this quality. My girlfriend and I had dinner reservations at a restaurant and we caught a show at the Kentucky Center for the Arts. We returned to the Brown Hotel around 11:30 PM.

Our room was fine, nothing was disturbed. Neither of us sensed anything paranormal.

I asked my girlfriend to select a bed for us to sleep in. My writer never indicated which bed she slept in and I never thought to ask. My girlfriend selected the bed on the north side of the room. We prepared for bed and we slept very well.

On Sunday morning, which was Valentine's Day, I woke up first. I started complaining to my girlfriend and accusing her of 'laying on my right arm, twisting my arm, and pulling on it.'

She roused up, and denied any of my accusation. She said she didn't pull, twist or lay on my right arm.

Then, she sat up in the bed and with a puzzled look, she said to me, 'Why were you biting on my right shoulder all night long?'

My girlfriend dropped back her gown, revealing her right shoulder. I could clearly see teeth marks all over the top, right shoulder.

I responded with, "I never once bit on your shoulder at all, you were pulling and twisting on my arm. Those aren't my teeth marks!"

"You were biting me," she said. "You were lying on my arm!"

We just stopped and looked at each other. We reached the same conclusion. That ghost, that aggressive spirit that had assaulted that woman, had decided to pay us a visit.

She was struck on the right side of her face, my right arm, and my girlfriend's right shoulder. We had both, been paid of visit by something menacing, something troubling that sure wanted to make its presence known to two unsuspecting guests.

Now, I don't believe that aggressive spirit was of Mr. Brown at all. But, with a hotel building that is 88 years old, it's just about impossible to have data on every single room within that building.

I can sympathize with the woman's pain of her being slapped and I can sympathize with my girlfriend's eerie teeth marks, but I sure can't understand it.

To preserve the integrity of the hotel and the privacy of future guests, only the E-mail writer and the author know the true locations of the actual rooms in question.

Voices From The Other Side at the Seelbach Hotel

One of my associates, Eve Edwards, is a psychic here in the Louisville area. We had met and shared the floor of entertainment on the Belle of Louisville back in June of 2013.

Eve Edwards had contacted me about wanting to walk my route with me, just to see if she could make any contact, or provide some additional information about the ghosts along my Louisville Ghost Walk route. I was excited about having a psychic on my tour and I was looking forward to any inside information she could provide. I told her that possibly, I could fill in any missing part of her narration that the spirits or ghosts provide her with.

We had reached the Seelbach Hotel. We were in the Old Seelbach Bar on the first floor trying to relax a bit and enjoying some cold water. I had previous shared with Eve about the bartender Cindy, who on previous occasions had had experiences with a ghost who kept calling her name once the bar had closed.

Cindy, the bartender, had told me that a male voice had called her name, and she would turn around, and nobody would be there. I provided Eve Edwards with that story and asked Eve if she thought any such ghost was in the bar.

"In a bar, I pick up on lots of negative energies, mostly because of the addictions that people succumb to inside of bars. Alcoholism, drug addictions, you name it, that negative energy can be overwhelming. However, concerning Cindy, I do feel as if a spirit is in here and his name is Jack.

"Jack was a frequent guest of the Seelbach Hotel, and most likely, had some type of a friendly relationship with Cindy.

"Unfortunately, Jack died and he still has a connection inside of the Old Seelbach Bar and apparently, some fascination with the bartender Cindy.

"When you get a chance, ask Cindy if she knew a previous guest of the hotel that she had served and was cordial with, and if his name was Jack, just to see what happens," Eve Edwards said.

I had mentioned to Eve Edwards about some of the reported ghosts of the Seelbach Hotel, and the one that's most famous being, The Lady in Blue. I asked Eve Edwards if she'd like to have a tour of the hotel and she agreed.

We had reached the 10th floor and once we stepped from the elevator, I realized right off that the 10th floor was under some summer time restoration and renovation. Ladders were out, paint cans, most of the window treatments were down from the corridors, and only a few of the hallway lights were lit. I'm familiar with the layout of the 10th floor, so I led the way.

I wanted Eve to see the Grand Ballroom first. Not only is that a wonderfully decorated room, but author F. Scott Fitzgerald had referenced it in his novel, The *Great Gatsby.*

Furniture was grouped together under one of the chandeliers in the foyer of the Grand Ballroom. Painting cans were canvassed and workmen had left their tools off to the side.

As I was pointing out some of the features of this historical room, I could hear male voices echoing from the hallway. I couldn't distinguish or hear clearly what the men were saying to each other, but it was apparent that men were talking down the darken hallway.

"Do you hear that?" I asked Eve. "There are some workmen up here working at this hour. Let's go find them and ask them if they've experienced anything ghostly."

I led the way down a dimly lit hallway. I could hear the male voices in the distance. We passed several locked doors. Once we reached the kosher kitchen, I pushed open the door and looked inside, and nobody was there.

Eve and I continued until we had reached a dead end fire door and the end of the hallway. The only thing that remained was a large window that had no curtains hanging at the glass, and it looked out onto the rooftops of neighboring building.

I turned to Eve and said, "That's funny; there's nobody here."

We turned around and walked back. I was puzzled. Eve remained silent as we walked.

Once we reached the foyer where we began, I stopped and said to Eve, "I know what I heard, which were voices of men, workmen, and they were down that hallway. I don't understand where they could have gone. It was if the men had just vanished. I know you heard them, too; it wasn't just me."

"Robert, I heard them too, but they weren't workmen," Eve said.

I looked at her with some confusion. "What are you talking about?" I asked.

"The voices you and I both heard, were ghosts! You heard ghosts in here," she said.

"Why didn't you tell me? Why didn't you say something before I took off down the hallway?" I asked her.

"Because you needed to experience hearing ghostly voices for yourself. I knew all along those were ghosts, but had I told you, it wouldn't have had the same impact on you. You needed to have investigated it for

yourself and then, come to the realization that the voices you heard weren't normal, human voices, but voices from the other side."

I turned and looked at the dark hallway, from which we had just come. Who was actually down the hallway that had something to say? And why were they there? It's a shame those men chose not to make their presence known to us in another way.

Waverly Hills Sanatorium Hospital

I'd like to share with the readers my experiences at Waverly Hills Sanatorium. Hospital. Most people are familiar with Waverly Hills, and they've heard plenty of the stories about how haunted the old building is, how sinister the building looks with the broken windows, and of the enormous number of deaths that have occurred in the building due to patients suffering with tuberculosis.

Waverly Hills Sanatorium is still considered to be one of the most haunted locations in all of North America, and it still attracts guests from all over the world.

If you're not familiar with Waverly Hills Sanatorium, this will provide you with some needed information that will help complete this story.

Waverly Hills Sanatorium operated as a tuberculosis hospital for fifty years off Dixie Highway in southwest Jefferson County. For some reason, the city of Louisville and Jefferson County had an alarming number of patients with tuberculosis, so the need was great for a facility to be built to treat these patients.

Construction began in 1908 and by 1911 it was finished and was ready to welcome the first eight patients. The patient population grew by an enormous amount, so during the years of 1924-26, the facility was enlarged. Infants, children, and adults found themselves in treatment at Waverly Hills Sanatorium. It was structured to have a playground on the 5th floor, a library, and school curriculum for the youngsters.

The community of Waverly Hills was self-sufficient. Employees, doctors, nurses, and their families lived on the premises. Church services occurred there by the Catholic and Protestant ministers. Crops were planted for fresh food, a grocery for patients and employees to shop was there, and the facility also published a patient and staff newsletter.

Tuberculosis came under control when the drug streptomycin became available. Waverly Hills Sanatorium's population declined and the doors were closed in 1961. The building was used by different groups and health care operations, but none seem to last very long. Rumors circulated among the community of the harsh treatments of those had loved ones there, when it was a nursing home and a facility for those with mental retardation. The last patient left in 1980.

But what about the patients who suffered with tuberculosis and met their death there? Sure, their bodies left, but could their spirits still be there?

That's what I wanted to know on my visit to Waverly Hills Sanatorium.

Over the past years of doing Louisville Ghost Walks, I've met countless individuals and groups who have booked tours with Waverly Hills Sanatorium and then went on my ghost walks. During our time together, I'd hear their stories and as time would allow, I'd share mine.

As a reader of this book, maybe you've had some Waverly Hills Sanatorium experiences. Maybe you want to experience Waverly Hills Sanatorium for yourself one day. I hope you'll enjoy what I have to share of my Waverly Hills experience.

I had just begun Louisville Ghost Walks. I had received support from Louisville Ghost Hunters and other friends who supported my efforts to tell the stories of ghostly Louisville's most famous addresses.

You've probably heard the expression 'through a friend of a friend'; well I managed to get an invitation using that format, of a friend of a friend. I was distantly involved with the Louisville Ghost Hunters group. I'm acquainted with founder Keith Age, and I knew he was hosting this group at Waverly Hills. I am also friends with storytellers, Lonnie and Roberta Simpson Brown. It was through their involvement with Louisville Ghost Hunters that I made the guest list. I was thrilled to have been included.

On this particular night in September, we had met at the Waverly Hills property. Waverly Hills was just a shell of a building. It was standing in ruin on that hillside in southwest Jefferson County. Vines covered the exterior. Vandals had broken out every window and trashed the building inside and out. Electricity was non-existent in the building. However, on our night, the hosts of this event had prepared for the guests on the tour a delicious meal that had been catered for the event. All kinds of people from the media were in the crowd that night. I recall folks representing Sci-fy, M-TV, and Discovery

Channel, as well as authors like Troy Taylor and others there. All of those people were new to me and I felt honored to be in their presence.

The tour into the building hadn't begun just yet. I had joined with Lonnie and Roberta Simpson Brown, and I wanted to tour the building with them. We had to enter the building from the backside, not the main entrance. We climbed one or two flights of stairs. As we assembled ourselves inside one of the hallways that would lead us to the dining hall, a very large door just slammed closed, right before our eyes! We all jumped and looked in disbelief at what had just happened. Nobody was anywhere near that door. By the shear weight of the door, there was no way wind or a draft could have caused something of that size to have slammed closed on it own.

The guide who was leading the tour just simply looked at the closed door and said, "Get used to it, doors slam closed in this building all the time."

The slamming of the door was quite unnerving. What else could be waiting for us in the ghostly looking five-story building? I remained in close contact with my friends, Lonnie and Roberta Simpson Brown. Our first location was the hospital-dining hall. Graffiti had marred the brick walls. Debris covered the floor, which made viewing the tiled floor difficult. The windows had no glass in the panels, so the building was an open-air type of a structure.

The facilitators had given us time to explore the cafeteria. From what history had recorded, the meals served at Waverly Hills were delicious meals that were served up by talented chefs. Another point was that the aroma of bacon and cinnamon rolls often filled the air of the old abandon cafeteria. The reality being, it had been decades since food had been prepared or even served in that room. Was that the traces of past spirits still roaming about and preparing breakfast? Or spirits following the aroma of food?

My friends and I had roamed about for about twenty minutes in the cafeteria. What I had noticed was the sudden drop in temperature in the room, but I discounted it being was September and the sun was beginning to set. That explained the coolness of the temperature.

It must have rained earlier in that day, since puddles were on the floor. Again, that would be expected inside of a deserted building without glass.

I had gathered with my friends when I felt the chill in the air. The temperature dropped suddenly. However, what caught my eye made a lasting impression upon me that I'd have to say became my very first, paranormal, ghostly experience ever.

A puddle of water was close by, yet, it wasn't disturbed at all. No ripples, no waves, nothing. On the floor and just inches from where we were standing the first foot print made contact with the floor. From my observation, something had made contact with the water that formed the puddle, and then, it placed its foot onto the floor and left the print. I could see the entire foot, and all five toes.

The ghost's footprints didn't stop there. The ghost was walking away from us! It was a left foot, followed by a right footprint, and then left. All in all, it was a total of five-foot prints. By the time the fifth footprint made contact with the floor, the final footprint left on the floor was the heel of the foot and part of the big toe.

We rushed around the footprints and looked in much disbelief as to what had just happened. But it was real and it had happened right before our eyes.

My group and I just assumed that it was the ghost of a female patient. After comparing the size of the footprints with our own feet, we assumed that it was female because men generally have much larger feet than the footprints that were now on the floor.

We also assumed that it was a patient, and not just a female nurse. At that time, nurses wouldn't have been elsewhere in the building barefooted, especially in the cafeteria. But a patient, possibly.

It didn't take long for the footprints to just evaporate into the air. The temperature returned to normal, so there was no longer a chill in the air.

And whoever 'she' was that evening strolling through the cafeteria, she had gotten her fill of the place and didn't return to see us, again. At least that we know of.

Welfare of Patients in a Fort Worth, Texas Hospital

I consider it a great opportunity and a compliment when guests on my tour like to linger around and share with me, some of their own personal ghost stories. At the conclusion of one walk, I had two women from Fort Worth, Texas, who were attending a convention here for nurses. Their schedule allowed them to walk with me one evening.

It just so happened on this particular night, we were caught up in a spring storm and rain fell on most of the walking tour. We remained dry by seeking shelter from the overhangs, awning, and marquees of the downtown buildings. The dark clouds and rain made for an eerie background for ghost stories. We had made it safely to the Seelbach Hotel where we were able to relax indoors on sofas on the mezzanine level and share stories as the rain pounded the pavement.

The ladies praised the tour and teased me about arranging the dark clouds and rain to help set the mood for the ghost stories. We all had a good laugh about that.

Barbara, a lady in her mid-50s, said she had been to Louisville before with the nursing convention, but had never been on my walk. Her traveling companion Lisa was new to the city and enjoyed the tour and history of Louisville's most famous addresses.

"Lisa and I both work in nursing in Fort Worth, Texas hospital," said Barbara.

"I'm not a big believer in ghosts, but I do enjoy the stories about the supernatural. I can't say I'm looking for anything scary happen to me that involve ghosts, but one incident does stand out in my mind that happened at the hospital where we both work."

Gesturing with her hands to include Lisa, Barbara said, "We both work in a neo-natal unit at the hospital. This happened just a couple years ago, when I was working in pediatrics at the hospital.

"A young boy named Timmy was one of the patients. Timmy was at least nine years old, cute fellow, with blond hair.

"Due to a terrible automobile accident, Timmy was on a ventilator and confined to his bed. He had been hospitalized for at least two years, so I was able to get to know him and his parents very well.

"Timmy had very little mobility, so we had to provide intense medical care, plus helping him with any movements in his bed. Timmy had to wear a tract in his throat for the ventilator.

"Timmy liked to jiggle his chin in this up and down motion. I think doing that made him laugh, and it was quite comical.

"Timmy also liked to pull this little trick, even though we cautioned him time and time again, not to do this for it was very dangerous. But, kids will be kids, and he had found this to be quite entertaining. I know he liked our reaction, and the attention this created, but he never realized the seriousness of this little trick.

"Timmy was able to hold his breath, just enough, to exhale air, which would cause the tract to pop out from the connection in his throat.

"Of course, the monitors would sound alarms, lights would blink, and we would come running to check on Timmy. He loved the attention that would cause. We would all scold him about doing that, and remind him of the dangers that could cause.

"One day it turned tragic. Timmy did his little routine of holding his breath and then exhaling. The tract popped out and the way it landed, it covered the opening, which prevented the monitor from sounding the alarm.

"Even though we were all in close range, nobody knew anything was wrong. A nurse was attending to a child just in the next bed, and she had no idea that Timmy was laying in the bed, just steps behind her, gasping for breath and slowly dying.

"Timmy suffocated and he couldn't get anyone's attention due to his inability to move or wave his arms around.

"It was too late for anything to be done; Timmy had died, by the result of his own practical joke that he liked to play.

"Timmy's bed was soon cleaned and his area was readied for a new patient. A number of weeks had passed before a new patient was assigned to that bed in the pediatrics area of the unit.

"A young girl named Abby was the next patient to use that space. Abby was a few years younger than Timmy, maybe seven years old. She was alert, and she had more mobility than Timmy. Abby was in the hospital recovering from an illness that almost ended her life.

"One day, Abby said to me, 'Who is that little boy that keeps hanging around my bed, and playing with my toys?'

"We have no children in the unit who are able to get up and walk around to visit with the other children on their own. If a child is up, he or she with either in a wheelchair, or is with one of the nurses or physical therapist, never up strolling without a nurse. The children are not able to get up and move about on their own.

"I just commented back that she must have been dreaming that no children are up playing, or visiting other children at their bedsides. She was quick to correct me and tell me yes, that a little boy comes to see her. He'll often sit on the side of her bed, touch her hand, or just stare at the blinking lights on the monitors.

"I just smiled, but without really giving it much thought, I asked her to describe this little boy.

"He's a blond haired boy, and he looks to be a little bigger than me. The more she described her bedside visitor, the more her description sounded just like Timmy. I stopped what I was doing, and I just stood there listening in amazement to what she was saying.

"The curiosity got to the best of me, and I had to ask her another question. I asked her, 'Has he ever said anything to you, like asking your name or telling you his name, or asking why you are here in the hospital?'

"I really wasn't expecting an answer, for I never really thought ghosts communicated with people, or that only happened in the Hollywood scripts.

"I could tell she was thinking. She took a deep breath, and said, "Timmy, I think he told me his name was Timmy. But, I've not seen him in a while.

"I was stunned, just shocked, for Timmy was the previous patient who died in that bed!

"The little girl said, 'I don't know if he'll ever come back to see me. He said he was going away and might not come back anymore.'

"I knew it wouldn't help her condition had I told her that a young boy named Timmy was once in that bed of the unit, and he had died. In fact, I never shared that information with her parents either. I don't know if she ever told her parents about that ghostly visitor she often had to keep her company.

"It wasn't long after that conversation, that Abby was moved from our unit. She was well enough to be moved elsewhere in the hospital, and I've not seen her since then.

"Maybe she'll take the memory of Timmy with her and not forget about him, and just think of the little blond haired boy who would stop by her bedside to visit.

"Lisa's got a story to tell you as well. I wouldn't say our hospital is haunted, but I think we have all had something that we just couldn't explain to happened to us when we're working with patients who are near death," said Barbara.

"The only time I encountered a ghost, was when I was working in a heart recovery patient area. I was taking care of an elderly woman named Wanda," said Lisa.

"Wanda had been hospitalized for a few days, but she was improving and would be discharged very soon. One of the nursing aides was helping me that morning in her room. Wanda had mentioned to me, and I just assumed it was the medicine doing the talking, but she said to me that during the morning, she had a dream, or a vision, and she was floating in the room, and from up above, she was looking down at her body. She said she wasn't in any pain and that she wasn't hooked up to the heart monitor or anything.

"Wanda told us about her vision as the nursing aide and I were giving her a bed bath. Everything was going okay and we were just about finished with the bath.

"Once finished in the bed, we had to move Wanda to the chair so we could replace the sheets with dry sheets.

"We got Wanda all seated and comfortable in the chair behind us. The aide and I were just chatting, making conversation with Wanda and putting the dry linens on the bed. But our focus wasn't really on watching Wanda, just getting the bed ready.

"Wanda said, 'I feel like I'm floating and I can see my body, laying right there in the bed.'

"The aide and I just exchanged smiles and glances as we smoothed out the bed linens, and one of us said something back to Wanda, like, we're just about finished here and you can get back into your bed.

"I turned around, to say something to her, and Wanda was dead! She had died right in the chair! Her final words were, "I feel like I'm floating and I can see my body, laying right there in the bed."

126

"I called for help and the aide and I did everything we could at the moment, but it was too late. Wanda had passed away, and her departing spirit seen her physical body, right there in the bed.

"All I can say is, at least Wanda wasn't alone when she died, nor was she in any pain. Her spirit just floated right up to the heavens," said Lisa.

"What Are You Doing?" Inquired a Ghost at the Seelbach Hotel

Louisville Ghost Walk concludes at the Seelbach Hotel. I take the guests inside and present the history and tell some of the ghost stories on the mezzanine level.

If the opportunity does present itself, I'll introduce my guests to any of the employees that are in the area who have had ghostly experiences.

As the title of this book, *Haunted Louisville 3...You're Never Alone,* this next story features an employee of the Seelbach. Jordan had an encounter on the 8th floor, that just proves to the readers that in a sense, 'you're never really alone' and that ghostly presence tend to be everywhere. Some just decide to make their presence known and in the most unusual of places. Or to the most unsuspecting person that happens to be in the right place at the right time.

Jordan is a young, college age man who's been with the hotel about two years. He works as a valet and doormen and escorting guests to their rooms. His story isn't one that I tell my guests, but if I see Jordan and he's not busy, I'll introduce him and encourage him to tell his story to my guests. I feel like they enjoy hearing accounts from actual employees who have had ghostly encounters and not just me, repeating what I've heard in my interviews.

Jordan had a few minutes, so he was able to tell my guests what had happened to him.

"I had been working here about one year, and I'd heard lots of things from the housekeeping staff and maintenance guys about ghosts, but nothing had ever happened to me.

"I had some luggage to take up to the room on the 8th floor; actually, it was 836 to be exact. Whoever rented the room wasn't around, but the luggage was on the cart and I had the room number.

"I boarded the elevator and made the delivery. I knocked on the door, and nobody answered. I knocked a second time, and still, no answer. So I used the passkey and went inside and dropped off the luggage.

"I was making my way back toward the elevators. This building has several hallways that turn and twist about the building when it was constructed in 1907. Some areas of the hallways are deserted.

"I had just rounded the corner when I heard a voice call out, 'What are you doing?' I stopped and looked around I didn't see anyone so I kept on going pushing the empty luggage cart.

"I just shook if off as overhearing a conversation from a room.

"Then he said it again, only it sounded a little more annoyed. The male voice called out, 'Where are you going?'

"I stopped and looked all around. Nobody was around at all. In fact, where I was standing on the hallway, there were no guests rooms, just in case I was hearing a conversation that was coming from inside. I was in one of those deserted areas.

"Yeah, I felt a little weird, I was hearing things, voices, from a guy who wasn't there.

"And what made it so weird was that I was walking. I'd changed areas of the hallway and the voice seemed to be following me.

"I stopped, and left the luggage cart. I walked all around the hallway area, and never saw anyone. I heard nothing coming from any guest's room like a television or anything, it was almost eerily quiet. Too quiet, if that's a good explanation.

"Once I got back to the luggage cart where I left it, I wasted no time and heading to the elevator. I thought that if the voice said anything else, I was just going to keep on going and not stop, nor look back.

"Who ever that guy was, I didn't want to see him, or hear him anymore. I didn't like any of the sensation that I was feeling and I just wanted to get off of the 8th floor."

I asked Jordan if he has any problem going to the 8th floor. He said that to this day, he doesn't like making runs to the 8th floor at all, especially on the southern side of the building.

"Whatever was there that day, might still be hanging around. Why he chose to speak to me remains a mystery as far as I'm concerned," said Jordan.

What I Could Hear, I Could Not See at Louisville Memorial Auditorium

Just a few blocks south of downtown on 4th and Kentucky Streets, stands an impressive building with Greek Doric columns across the front. The citizens of Louisville discussed ways to honor those who had fought and died in the war, on Armistice Day, 1929, so the building known as Louisville Memorial Auditorium opened its doors.

"Erected by the citizens of the city of Louisville and the county of Jefferson in memory of their soldiers, sailors, and marines, who served the nation in World War," are the words written on a plaque on the building.

The interior hallways are lined with 144 famous flags flown in World Wars I and II, plus personal banners and flags of famous American generals. Those remembrances of men and their heroic deeds are easy to understand and to connect to, but what about ghosts that could be stirring about in some level of remembrance?

I sing with the Louisville based Thoroughbred Chorus and we hold our annual Christmas show at the Memorial Auditorium the first weekend in December. Some of the ladies whose husbands sing in the all male chorus use the lobby as an area for refreshments and beverages before the show, intermission, and afterwards. The ladies lend their talents to set up nice displays of food and holiday treats and beverages. However, during the show only one or two ladies remain in the lobby area, while the others go into the auditorium to relax a bit and enjoy the singing of the Thoroughbred Chorus.

One of the members' wives had this to share with me after our last performance in December 2013. Her name is Rita Hardin and I've known her for several years. I believe in her testimony.

"I was in the lobby alone, everyone else had gone into auditorium," Rita said.

"The show was in progress and I could hear the singing and then, applause.

"As I was just moving about the tables, taking care of the food items and cleaning up from the food being served prior to the show, something caught my eye.

"I wasn't expecting to see a man standing there but he was just there, just across the room.

"He didn't last long at all, but he faded from sight. He was visible long enough to catch my attention. He didn't move my way at all, but I know that was a ghost.

"I do believe in ghosts and other things in the paranormal realm, so it really didn't bother nor surprise me at all to spot a ghost in the lobby. When I looked up again, he was gone.

"I went about my duties, moving from table to table, arranging the food and cleaning up, just thinking some about the ghost that I'd just seen.

"Apparently, he must have read my mind, for he returned just a few minutes later, appearing in a new location of the lobby. This time, he appeared a little closer to where I was now standing.

"I couldn't really distinguish if he was in military clothing or just street clothes, but I kept looking at him with glances toward him. I thought it best, to just go about my business and act normal and not make any reactions his way. I wanted to see more of him, but I didn't want him to see me staring at him.

"The third time I looked up and glanced his way, he was gone.

"I decided to walk over his way to just look around, and to double check that I wasn't seeing anyone's reflection in the marble flooring or walls. In his area, nobody was there, and since all the doors and curtains were drawn that led into the auditorium, I ruled out any shadows."

Now I've performed on that stage for several holiday performances. I love exploring and just being in the spotlight. I think about all the big-names who have graced that 85 foot stage, names like George Gershwin, Helen Hayes, George M. Cohan, and Marian Anderson, all have left their imprints, their personalities on that stage on which I have stood. But are others, less famous still hanging about the stage and back stage areas? I tend to think so and often wonder who else might be hanging about the building.

On the upper floor of the building, houses the Skylight Ballroom. Most people just refer to this location as the banquet room and that is where the chorus holds its cast parties after each show. But I hope to revitalize its name, the Skylight Balloon, because of the large, three skylights that would illuminate the room.

On the night of our performance, we had our cast party in the Skylight Ballroom. The room is rectangular in shape, with wooden paneling and sections of carpeted and marble floor.

I was seated at the table with Rita Hardin, and her husband Harry, as well as several others from the chorus. Rita Hardin and I were across the table from each other. In the Skylight Ballroom is where Rita shared with me about the ghostly experienced she had witnessed downstairs.

As our conversation progressed, I mentioned to Rita and the others at our table, that even though we have this room just about filled with chorus members, spouses, and other entertainers who performed with us earlier, other ghosts are up here. At first, even with the dim lighting and people moving about I could see 'additional' guests entering and exiting from the distant doorway on the opposite side. Those guests, were all in the pale gray appearance and only lasted fleeting seconds, long enough for the human eye to perceive something, process it, and then try to identify it as a living person. Some appeared to be dancing, while others appeared to just be moving across the floor. Their presence only lasting for seconds only. Physical features were impossible to identify, nor could any time period be assigned. But at this midnight hour, the sounds of laughter, applause, and singing most likely, invited entertainers and guests from that by-gone era of stage life, to rejoin this party in their ghostly splendor and glory.

I remained at the cast party until 1 a.m. and said my good-byes and good nights to everyone. When I left the Skylight Ballroom, I closed the door behind me from the third floor and I could no longer hear the laugher and singing from the chorus. I exited down a back staircase alone until I reached the main floor.

As I was descending the gray, concrete steps, I could tell that I was being followed. With each landing, I had to make a 90-degree turn to reach the next set of stairs, and I could hear footsteps, those like heels or dancing shoes with patent leather soles following behind me. But as I'd look upwards and downwards, I saw nothing; but I know what I heard. What I could hear, I could not see, yet, it was making its presence known.

I can only hope that a ghost from one of those long, forgotten cast parties had decided to exit with me. Maybe that ghost was ready to return to the stage for one more late night appearance.

About the Author:

Robert Parker, author of the two previous Haunted Louisville books, has just completed his third, Haunted Louisville 3....You're Not Alone and has enjoyed working on this project. Not only does Robert Parker find pleasure in interviewing people who have ghostly encounters to share, he finds pleasure in walking and touring their property in hopes of having his own ghostly encounter there. Robert Parker remains busy in the local community with a wide range of activities and interests, such as being a five-year worker with the Kentucky Derby Festival with emphasis on the Pegasus Parade. Robert Parker also is concerned about community issues and volunteers one night a week serving the homeless population in the city with food, water, first-aid supplies and above all us, friendship. Robert Parker has enrolled in cooking classes and considers himself to be one of the new 'foodies' among his friends and is always in search of a good meal. With future plans after retirement with the local board of education, he plans to teach cooking classes in the local area and still remain in education. He also plans to visit all fifty states and explore haunted locations, and tour as many of our nation's national parks as possible.

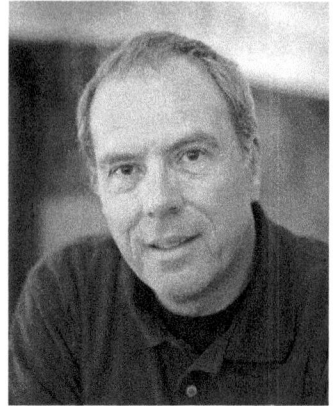

About the Photographer:

Justin Coulter completed the photography for the second book authored by Parker, so he was thrilled to provide the photography for this third book. This is Justin's second professional photography assignment in publication. When not taking photographs, Justin is the president of the Derby City Jeep Club in Louisville and is focused on charity fundraising and keeping the jeep club active in the community. Justin and his wife Casi Mason Coulter, reside in Mt. Washington, Kentucky, and enjoy taking care of their dog, Dutch, and their two cats. Justin and his wife value spending time with family and friends, and many outdoor activities. Justin also enjoys all types of photography, from weddings, portraiture, to fine art, architecture and still life. To see more of the photographer's work, please visit www.jcoulterphotography.com

About Louisville Ghost Walks:

Louisville Ghost Walks is in its 12th year of ghost and history tour service. Guests have found their way to this legendary ghost story program of downtown Louisville's most famous addresses. Guests have represented all fifty states in our country, represented foreign countries of London, England, Sweden, Brazil, and as far away as New Zealand and Australia, and have been enthralled with the stories presented by Mr. Ghost Walker. The common thread is that no matter the state, or foreign country, the paranormal exists in each culture.

As I tell my guests, for there to be a haunting, their must be a connection for that ghost to remain. The connection can be a simple guardian spirit, a protector, or someone who just doesn't know he or she has passed on. Other ghosts could remain because they feel as if they have unfinished business, or in the worse case, an untimely death.

When time allows and my guests share with me their stories and their experiences of the paranormal, stories that they have carried with them in their memories, all have that same element as I share with my guests who walk with me on Louisville Ghost Walks. Each person has a story to tell. Some are more vocal than others and like to share. Some like to keep their own personal stories as their own private experiences to hold dear to their hearts. Those experiences shape each person and help form their own views on the paranormal.

That's what Louisville Ghost Walks is all about, sharing those stories that have been told to Mr. Ghost Walker, and hearing those personal accounts from him and other business people, employees, and owners of the buildings in the downtown district.

Next time you're in the city of Louisville, consider joining Mr. Ghost Walker on one of his downtown ghost walking tours, and find out for yourself, that as the title reminds each person, that, 'You're Not Alone'

Louisville Ghost Walks
Tours Friday and Saturday nights or by appointment during the week
Contact: 502-689-5117
Web: www.louisvilleghostwalks.com
Email: LouGhstWalks@aol.com

The Locations:

People love the thrill of hearing ghost stories of factual people, and many folks enjoy taking a short trip to visit a location that is reported to be haunted. If you're so inclined to visit some of the places that I've written about in this book and want to tour them yourselves, I've included the addresses. As with any business, please use discretion and get permission from the owner if you'd like to check out the property and conduct your own personal, ghost investigation. Happy hauntings!

- Brown Hotel, 335 West Broadway, 502-583-1234
- Culberson Mansion Historic Home, 914 East Main   Street, New Albany, Indiana,
- 812-944-9600
- DiFabio Casapela Italian Restaurant 2311 Frankfort Avenue, 502-891-0411
- Dish-on-Market, 434 West Market, 502-315-0669
- Frazier Historical Arms Museum, 829 West Main Street, 502-753-5663
- Heyburn Building, 332 West Broadway, 502-585-2555
- Macy's Department Store, 7900 Shelbyville Road, Oxmoor Mall
- Memorial Auditorium, 970 South 4th Street, 502-584-4911
- Miss C's on Chestnut, 308 West Chestnut Street, 502-992-3166
- Patrick O'Shea's Pub, 123 West Main Street, 502-708-2488
- Seelbach Hotel, 500 South 4th Street, 502-585-3200
- Southern Middle School, 4530 Bellevue Avenue
- Waverly Sanatorium, 4400 Paralee Lane, 502-933-2142

www.ingramcontent.com/pod-product-compliance
Lightning Source LLC
LaVergne TN
LVHW051744080426
835511LV00018B/3214